Letters to the Grandchildren

Dedication

Many thanks to
Elizabeth Boleman-Herring, Wayne Chapman,
John Morgenstern, John Idol,
Harold Woodell, Ray Barfield, Ron Moran,
Anja, Brook, Shane, Aimee,
Edgar, Sterling, Spencer, Lena,
and, of course, Ingrid,
who kept the bandages, tissues,
and encouragement flowing.

Letters to the Grandchildren

by Skip Eisiminger

CLEMSON UNIVERSITY PRESS

Copyright 2014 by Clemson University
ISBN: 978-0-9890826-6-2

Published by Clemson University in Clemson, South Carolina.

Editorial Assistants: Chelsea Green and Dustin Mosley

Cover Designer: Chelsea Green

To order copies, please visit the Clemson University Press website: www.clemson.edu/press.

Contents

Our Common Bond

People Are Our Teachers

Foreword

After Skip Eisiminger's mother falsely accused him of forgetting a birthday some thirty years ago, he started documenting life's minor milestones on note cards, maintained in a six-inch wooden box. This modest container soon gave way to three, eighteen-inch boxes, which have since swelled to five, four-foot steel cabinets containing as many as 70,000 cards recording more than 400,000 items. No doubt Eisiminger's office resembles that of Fulgence Tapir, the bespectacled scholar of Anatole France's satirical novel *Penguin Isle*, who is swept away in a deluge of note cards cascading from the shelves of his own study. Yet, wholly unlike Tapir's cards, which record a series of cold facts, Eisiminger's cabinets overflow with life, including a three-inch file on "Love," a four-inch file on "Death," and the bountiful and wide-ranging experiences that make up everything in between. Drawing on these files, *Letters to the Grandchildren* showcases a wide array of thought-provoking meditations of universal appeal on the essential questions of how to love, how to learn, and above all, how to live.

Narrated with an irreverent wit comparable to only the finest humorists, many of these essays inform as well as delight, imparting practical approaches to teaching and learning both inside and outside the classroom. Developed over the course of a forty-year teaching career, Eisiminger's "Classroom Commandments," for instance, hands down hard-earned wisdom with an intelligence and thoughtfulness characteristic of the entire collection. While some of these recommendations apply more exclusively to academia, such as "Kill them with work and they'll die educated," many of these commandments are more broadly applicable to all walks of life: "Show up and give a cluck," "No dumbing down," "Make them laugh 3–4 times per hour," "Consider that you might be wrong," and "Assume the best until you know otherwise." Here and throughout, these life lessons are conveyed with the vivid wordplay of a true Idiom Savant and the clarion honesty of a grandfather addressing the generations.

Essays that address lessons outside of the classroom are at once erudite and accessible, raucously witty, and at times deeply heartwarming. A touching and memorable anecdote surely befitting of both Eisiminger's "Love" and "Death" folders comes in an essay that recounts the months following his father-in-law's passing. Inspired by the inscription "Objects in mirror are closer than they appear" on the rearview mirror of his Toyota Camry, Eisiminger reflects on the process of looking back while moving forward in the face of loss. Shrewdly discerning the toll of this loss on his wife, he reaches out to her by way of a Post-It stuck to her cosmetic mirror reading, "Objects in mirror are more beautiful than they appear." The following day, he finds a note taped to his shaving mirror bearing the words, "Objects in this mirror are smarter than I realized." The same conclusion might be drawn from the entirety of the *letters* collected in this volume: however lighthearted Eisiminger makes them seem, they reflect on questions that are indeed closer to each of us than they might at first appear.

John D. Morgenstern
Clemson, South Carolina, 2014

Introduction

Though I've long been what Rilke called an "internal gardener," I acquired the habit of keeping a commonplace book quite by accident. In the 1970s, I often taught one interdisciplinary humanities class, one composition class, and two literature classes each semester. The paintings in the humanities, the essays in the composition, and the fiction in the literature often had broadly overlapping themes like love and death. To prevent myself from sounding like a scratched CD, I started keeping a journal containing insights from Cicero to Erma Bombeck. These I copied out or cut and pasted into a bound notebook. The books, however, quickly grew so voluminous it took hours to locate the two-inch item I was searching for. I, therefore, shifted to an eight and a half by eleven inch vertical-file format, but by 1975 BC (Before Computers) my "Love" file was three inches thick; "Death" was four. Clearly I needed an information system that would better serve my classroom and research needs. That was when I recalled a professor at Auburn who had casually mentioned that he kept summaries of every scholarly article he read on one or more three by five inch cards.

Eventually the twenty big-theme files like "Love" and "Death" were refined and subdivided into 2200 card-file categories. I kept the vertical files, but beginning about 1980, I began funneling most of my clippings (which my German wife calls *schnippels*) into the card file.

After retiring in 2007, I often questioned the momentum that kept me maintaining the card file until I was contacted by a former Clemson colleague. Elizabeth Boleman-Herring, now living in New Jersey, asked if I'd be interested in writing a weekly column for *OfficialWire,* an online magazine that featured articles on everything from politics to the arts. I wrote for *OW* until late 2009, when the British-American-Greek owner cashiered several of us before being arrested by Scotland Yard on fraud charges. Those charges remain a mystery because neither Elizabeth nor I were ever paid for any work we did for *OW.* On the rebound, Elizabeth asked a half dozen of us if we would like to join her in another idealistic, online enterprise, *Weekly Hubris.* Over the next three years, I wrote more than two hundred, 1000-word personal essays, each based on one of the topics in my card file. To date, I'm two thousand short of completion.

While writing these essays, both of my parents died. When I read that Cicero had left his son a series of brief personal "letters," I was disappointed that my parents had not done something similar. That's when I decided to learn from the "sin" of their omission and salt away some of my essays in a book.

Arthur Schopenhauer said that given our "three score and ten" allotment, a wise division would be forty years devoted to the "text" and thirty to the "commentary." My division thus far has been rather less balanced—sixty-five for the text and six for the commentary, but at least I've managed to get a few things in print before shuffling off to Buffalo dragging my mortal coil. To switch the metaphor, I've spent the last six years unpeeling a very large onion. In the process, I've cut my fingers numerous times and occasionally brought tears to my eyes, but once sautéed with a little butter, the result, I think, is a palatable dish. *Guten Appetit!*

Skip Eisiminger
Clemson, South Carolina, 2014

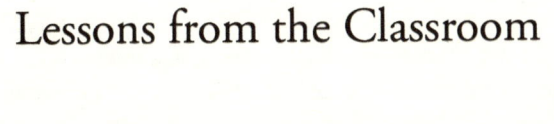
Lessons from the Classroom

The Office Door: Introductions

"Solomon, Solomon, have you no sons?"
—Anonymous

"Don't nobody don't like Dr. E."
—Anonymous student

*O*ver the forty years I taught English and humanities at Clemson University, students arriving at my door in Strode Tower were greeted by a bewildering array of passive-aggressive cartoons, photographs, and quotations. These were taped, glued, and thumb tacked to my door, door frame, and bulletin board. I'm not sure where the impulse arose, but it might have been Emerson's advice to write "whim" on the lintels of the door posts. I had no such romantic pretensions; I only wanted to introduce myself to those waiting for an audience in my chambers. Many times, I arrived, and finding students reading my door, I was reluctant to interrupt them. Often they were not my own, but I was always pleased that someone was paying attention to this vast, conceptual "work in progress." When I retired from full-time teaching, I used a razor blade to peel off each of the 754 items, which I then compulsively glued to thirty-nine 3x5 cards.

These cards are now in my file where one day someone will have a ready supply of material for a biography or elegy. But as I filed the cards under "Skip," I thought, "Why should someone else have all the fun?" So I decided to write an essay based on the quotes, some original but most not, that I once chose for their humor, truth, or both. To acquire a little distance from myself, I've chosen to write in the third person.

Skip's office in 808 Strode Tower was alternately known as "Chateâu Bubba," the "Info Barn," "Logotopia," and the "Free-Speech Zone." Apparently this professor that some knew as "Thesaurus Rex" and "Dr. Verbivore" loved words at all levels of the language hierarchy as much as he loved prattling about them.

The "Cyber Ghetto," another nickname for 808, suggests that Skip was not on the leading edge of computer technology. By his own admission, he was, "Techno Amish," "User Surly," and a "Pothole on the Information Highway." As the millennium neared, he posted one irreverent clipping that said "Y2K=666." He also claimed to be "Teledildonic," but he will leave that to the reader to interpret. Perhaps he had powers no one appreciated or was simply handy with a remote.

Just as his office had nicknames, so did he. These included "Conan the Librarian," "Hugh Manatees," the "Tenured Seasquirt," the "Idiom Savant," "Dr. Lanky Shanks," the "Snackolator," the "Lallaperuser," and "Mensch." John Idol, one of Skip's colleagues and an early mentor, remembers him as the "Ad Hoc Director of Morale," and certainly many of his nicknames suggest that he was an optimist at heart, a rare quality in a satirist. Other nicknames like "Smut Warrior," "Prof. Tad Nitpicky," and the "Tenured Iconoclast" suggest that he had his issues with the world. To be sure, the department had its issues with him as will become clear.

Students and colleagues entering 808 were given fair warning that the "old-time religion" was off limits. Visitors were informed that Dr. E. was a "Foxhole Christian touched by an anvil," a "Non-Dogmatic Spiritualist," a "Barn-Again Theo-Nazi," a "Pulpit Bully," and a "Spiritual Green Beret." Ironically, Skip claimed that he just showed up to let the Lord work through him, and in the event of the Rapture, his office would be empty. When his department head asked him how religiously conservative students might respond to Skip's claim to be Beelzebubba, Skip answered with a versified posting, "Whether Christian, Muslim, or Jew, / the god in me greets the God in you."

A hint of Skip's "non-dogmatic spirituality" is found in the quotation, "Thank God it's Monday," because he loved what he did in 808 and the classrooms of Daniel Hall. His affections and concerns were often expressed in the advice he dispensed: "Give more and expect less," "Professors are not a luxury," "Eat less and excrete more," "Beware the high cost of low living," "Don't wait for people to love you," and, "You have a friend in exegesis." A man of few words, Skip's longest statement of advice observed two laws: "The Law of Science: what goes up must come down," and, "The Law of Faith: what goes down must come up."

At the core of Skip's pedagogical beliefs were his "Classroom Commandments":

- Show up and give a cluck.
- Make it seductive and they'll teach themselves.
- Do the worst first.
- Love your dictionary.
- If you're boring yourself, imagine how the rest feel.
- No dumbing down.
- Forward into the past, not backward into the future.
- Make them laugh 3–4 times per hour.
- Consider that you might be wrong.
- If you cannot persuade, insinuate.

• It's not the eloquence; it's the evidence.
•Assume the best until you know otherwise.
• Kill them with work and they'll die educated.

For all the chutzpa it must have taken to post his commandments, Skip had a self-deprecating streak as well. Who else would refer to himself on the same bulletin board as a "Global Village Idiot," "Professor Chuckle Trousers," "Internationally Ignored," a "Common Crossword Mistake," and "Dr. Awkward, Professor of Palindromic Studies"? Usually hip to the latest popular culture, Skip was "the weakest link," and a few years later, "most likely to be voted off the island."

A lifelong liberal independent, Skip usually voted Democratic though there were times he could not bear to vote for any candidate. When Vice President Dan Quayle told a seventh grader he'd misspelled "potato," Skip posted a note saying he was "orthographically sensitive to basic tubers." When President George W. Bush defined "the axis of evil," Skip proclaimed that he belonged to "the axis of the medieval." And when the National Rifle Association scored another victory for the gun-impoverished, Skip said he supported "the right to arm bears."

Because he taught the structure of poetry and the poetry workshop courses, many snippets referred to Skip's alter ego, "Busta Rhyme." He was alternately a "No-Holds Bard," the "Bubba Laureate," and the "Poet Lariat." He claimed that "Panic is my muse," "The early bard gets the word," and "Poetry slams are off limits." Assuming his fledgling versifiers would understand, he wrote, "Ye nymphs of Bath, prepare the lay." Again the department head appeared at the controversial portal with news that a woman in Busta's class was unhappy.

Skip walked to his door and pointed to the following, "In goddess we trust," "Anonymous was a woman," "Chicks rule," and "Men are pigs, but you can't kill them." After making a note of the last item for his wife, the boss advised Skip to take down the nymph reference. Reluctantly he did and also took down, "Welcome Kickboxing Geishas," not because it was sexist; it just wasn't drawing any business.

As long time colleague Claire Caskey said, "Skip was an aardvark always poking around for one more pismire." He didn't always succeed, but as Albert Holt, another colleague said, "Skip *tried* to make poems out of every damn thing."

When Skip retired from full-time teaching in 2007, he moved three floors down to the "Emeritus Office." After three years of part-time work, reports say that his half of the shared bulletin board is full.

Microcosms in the Classroom: Student Surnames

"What's in a name? That which we call a rose
By any other name would smell as sweet."
—William Shakespeare's Juliet

"He said true things but called them by the wrong name."
—Elizabeth Barrett-Browning

Ever since the Christmas my wife and children gave me the Dictionary of Surnames (Oxford UP, 1988), I have told my captive audiences where their names originated. Typically after a broad discussion of naming practices in a humanities class, I enjoyed surprising students with a brief explanation of their surnames. (Some of the names herein have been altered to protect the proprietors.) If Oxford or Google did not have an explanation, which happens about 10% of the time, I reported on a student's first or middle name, not to appear empty-handed. One year, I struggled with a Miss Lara Lack's surname. She'd told me that her family had emigrated from Russia in the late nineteenth century, but none of my resources—including a woman who teaches Russian—were any help. In class, after apologizing for my failure, the student said, "I should have told you that when my grandparents emigrated, some clerk at Ellis Island was unable to make heads or tails of Lachiskaia, so for lack of a better name, we became the Lack family."

Over the years that I've been rummaging through the name drawer, I've been consistently struck by the way most of my classes offer a neat microcosm of medieval culture. Occasionally a Korean like Kyungsun Kim or a Nigerian like Karla Kika Kuudjiku sneaks into the lineup, which is fine, of course, but usually my mostly Southeastern American students reflect a European heritage. A few years ago, I taught a young Muslim woman from Malaysia named Norbaya B.T. Hj Katana. As soon as I had a decent chance, I asked her about her puzzling name. She said basically it means, "I am Norbaya, the daughter of [B.T.] Mr. Katana, who has been on a hajj [Hj] to Mecca."

Unfortunately, most American names do not present such a detailed narrative, but they do have fascinations of their own. One young man whose family came from northern Italy is named John Sinisgaulli. I asked him if he knew the origin of his last name, and he said he'd asked his parents and grandparents, but no one knew. I told him there was a good chance his ur-ancestor was a left-handed interloper from France. Whether he'd been to Mecca is unrecorded. Another former student, States Rights Jaworski, has a name that reveals far more about his parents' political leanings than a Polish surname meaning "one who lives beneath a sycamore tree." It's a fair guess that his folks haven't been to Mecca either.

In September of 2010, I undertook my name exercise one more time before retiring. True to form, the microcosm I'd learned to expect over the last twenty years reappeared. In a class of thirty, I discovered fifteen English, six German, four French-Norman, three Norse, and two Scotch-Irish names. Over half the names were about evenly divided between the habitation and occupational types with ornamental, patronymic, and saintly allusions filling in the remainder. In the early twenty-first century, I had before me relatives of a fourteenth-century tool sharpener ("Whetzel"), a wrestler ("Resler"), two soldiers ("Bowman" and "Finley"), an innkeeper ("Hosler"), a mountain dweller ("Berglund"), a harness maker ("Burrell"), a church warden ("Sexton"), a wheelwright ("Wright"), a barrel maker ("Cooperman"), two servants ("McElhaney" and "Hall"), a former mayor ("Moyer"), two farmers ("Fields" and "Ackermann"), a forester ("Kiefer"), and three admirers of the saints Martin, Hugh, and Cannock. I also had the great (multiplied by twenty-five) grandchildren of William, Hain, John, and Rolf's sons. I had students with DNA from families who'd once lived in LeMans and Lyon, France; Halle, Germany; and Devonshire, England. I had relatives of those who'd made their living as a cherry orchardist in Germany, a hay farmer in Wales, and a woodcutter in Ireland. Indeed, I had a roomful of English majors studying the history of their language, and most of them were not even aware that they were carrying Old and Middle English scraps of a great tattered quilt.

Despite the work I put into the class on names, many students want to see for themselves what Oxford has to say, and I can't say that I blame them. Many have been told by grandparents some story conflicting with Oxford, so I always bring my dictionary to class and pass it around for the skeptical and curious to peruse. I tell them to be sure to read all the possibilities because many names have more than one origin. When that occurs, I usually pick the most flattering to broadcast. In the case of Mr. Burrell, the harness maker, Oxford also says some of the Burrells were "judicial torturers." After class, Mr. Burrell came by to tell me that he did not blame me for the information Oxford had imparted, for he was accustomed to being teased about his name. Because he carried the same name as his father and grandfather, his friends dubbed him "da turd."

Perhaps the most difficult moment when speaking of student surnames comes when dealing with the African-American names. In 2009, I had three such names: a Chapman, whose name is Middle or Old English for a merchant; a Fielding, whose Middle English name refers to one living on land cleared of the forest but not yet plowed; and a Koon, whose Irish name described a comely man. Since I am unaware of any Africans living in Great Britain in the fourteenth and fifteenth centuries when most Englishmen were required by law to take surnames, "Chapman," "Fielding," and "Koon" presented a problem. I asked the students in question if they or their parents had traced the family's name to a time before the 1863 emancipation, and all said that no one they knew of had been successful though several had tried. Young Mr. Koon volunteered that he was "James Koon the IV" and despite the bitter irony inherent in his name, he had no intention of changing a relict his ancestors had borne with dignity for 150 years.

I said I understood. As a resident of South Carolina, I was a Sandlapper like him and four million others. Though the nickname originated to describe people so poor they had to eat sand or clay to fill their bellies, I had no intention of moving to another state because some had been forced into geophagy. "Sandlapper" today, like the Koon surname, is a proud survivor of worse times in Ireland and the United States. Sometimes we forget that progress is real, and our names offer some of the best evidence we have of it.

The Emperor Is Naked: Deconstructionism

"Always remember that there is no city in Europe which contains a statue to a critic."
—Jean Sibelius

"A professional critic is a man who in dealing with a work of art, creates a little work of art in its honor."
—John Crowe Ransom

On October 11, 2004, I read a longish obituary of Jacques Derrida, the famed French deconstructionist critic who had generated tsunamis in the literary world's teacup for the past three decades. At the end of the article, the *New York Times* writer opted to give his readers a sample of Derrida's prose to illustrate a key idea from one of his final interviews collected in *Philosophy in a Time of Terror* (University of Chicago Press, 2003):

> We do not in fact know what we are saying or naming in this way: September 11, *le 11 septembre*, September 11. The brevity of the appellation (September 11, 9/11) stems not only from an economic or rhetorical necessity. The telegram of this metonymy—a name, a number—points out the unqualifiable by recognizing that we do not recognize or even cognize, that we do not yet know how to qualify, that we do not know what we are talking about.

Though I feared that Derrida had finally (in the words of Hobbes of *Calvin and Hobbes*) "made language a complete impediment to understanding," I asked a colleague who teaches literary theory for a loan of the full text, thinking that a little more context might be helpful. It wasn't. The *Times'* journalist had chosen well; he was not to blame for the stuttering repetitions, forced humor, fractured syntax, and other infelicities in Derrida any more than Derrida was responsible for what seems to me the denotative clarity of "9-11." Indeed, the term is so popular and expressive that it was chosen by the American Dialect Association as its "Word of the Year" in 2001. A Google search in November of 2005 turned up 85,100,000 hits, and by September 2011, this number had risen to 555,000,000. This sixfold increase should surprise no one given that the wars in Afghanistan and Iraq, two bitterly fought presidential elections, and the high-profile rebuilding in Washington and New York have kept the term on the cusp of our collective memory lobe over the last decade.

Assisting in our recall efforts is the coincidental fact that 911 is the country's emergency telephone number. I'd love to know if the date was chosen by the terrorists for its anxiety-laden connotations, but to the best of my knowledge, it wasn't, nor was it chosen because the number eleven resembled the Twin Towers. (See snopes.com for more in this rich vein.) Intentional or not, the term quickly picked up associations of horror in the West even as it became a rallying cry in many Muslim communities sympathetic to Al Qaeda. Of course, for many conservatives and a few militant liberals like me, it became a call to common action here as well. "9-11" to many of us was as clear a reason to go to war as any in history. Afghanistan, at least, was no War of Jenkins's Ear; Iraq was another story.

Before dismissing Derrida's objections as the uninformed ramblings of a foreign speaker, I decided to ask a class of mostly senior English majors to recast in their own words and comment on the passage above while I did the same myself. Here's my own paraphrase: The world refers to the terrorist attacks and the resulting loss of some three thousand lives in New York, Washington, and Pennsylvania on September 11, 2001 as "9-11." A natural desire for economy and effectiveness of expression is the main reason we have adopted it. But the truncated and somewhat cryptic term reveals our inability to ever know and characterize both what happened on that fateful day and why. Indeed, we do not know what we are talking about when we use "9-11."

Everyone in my class of thirty thought that Derrida had the denotation of "9-11" correct, and half agreed with his implied accusations: namely that "9-11" is "inadequate," "premature," "emotionless," "vague," and, in one case, "a rank euphemism." One student thought the term had convinced a majority of Americans to go to war, accusing the Bush administration of turning "9-11" into a "shrill jingoistic cry" like "Remember the Maine," or, "Remember the Alamo." But one shouldn't blame the term for the way it is used or misused. There's nothing intrinsic in "9-11" (or for that matter "the Holocaust" and "Pearl Harbor") that lends itself to manipulation or distortion. To me the denotation is abundantly clear; connotations naturally and inevitably will vary. But saying that "9-11" is inherently a war cry is like blaming "Christmas" and "the 4th of July" for implying commercialism and pomposity respectively. In the latter case, the blame belongs solely to those bandstand orators over the last two hundred years who have let their love of country cloud their better judgment.

According to one student, Derrida's chief objection to "9-11" was its prematurity: "we adopted this term without due consideration," she thought. When this point was discussed in class, I said that people of all cultures traditionally name the baby at birth or shortly thereafter. In some societies, people get a new name after an initiation or confirmation, but the new name may need adjustments, and the old is seldom discarded without regret. Indeed, "9-11" might change if there's a larger tragedy on some future September 11th the way "The Great War" became "World War I" in the 1940s as fifty-five million lay dead or dying. Personally, I cannot fault anyone for quickly adopting the term. Effective discourse demanded that we name it something; we did, it stuck, and it's not going away. Can 555,000,000 usages all be wrong?

As for "9-11" being "a rank euphemism," I'd have to disagree as well. There are circumlocutions and there are roundabout expressions, but in the worst sense ("guestage" for "hostage"), euphemisms are criminally evasive, subterfuges that seek to obscure something offensive or false for all the wrong reasons. (Recall, for example, Adolf Eichmann saying at his trial that he was "an expert on migration problems.") Personally, I find no felonious intent in "9-11." Had we dubbed the tragedy "Bush's Blooper," we would have deserved all the scorn we surely would have received. It's possible the tragedy might have been called "World Trade Center" or "WTC" or "Ground Zero" tying the tragedy to the place rather than the time, but "9-11" has a natural trochaic rhythm that "WTC" lacks. Plus the latter ignores what happened in Washington and Pennsylvania. Should the term allude to the mangled bodies more directly? In fact, "Bloody Tuesday" has been used 6,430 times according to Google in connection with "9-11"—a far cry from 555,000,000.

As for the term being shortened to a fault, I would remind these critics of Zipf's Law and point them to Maya Lin's Vietnam War Memorial in Washington, DC, especially now juxtaposed as it is with that affectation of grandeur, the World War II Monument, across the Mall. The understatement of Lin's triangular slabs of black marble plowing their way to a halt in some of this nation's most hallowed ground is possibly the most moving memorial ever created. Few who have visited it have left dry-eyed. What better way to commemorate the dead in a war that America lost than inscribe the names of the 58,000 fallen on a figurative instrument of frustration and hopelessness? "9-11" has the same poignant simplicity with its overtones of a fumbled emergency call while a loved one lies gasping at the caller's feet.

One student who disagreed with Derrida's brusque dismissal of "9-11" thought it was a haiku, a rough stone dropped into the well of her consciousness that brought up reminders of the New York firemen, the leadership of Mayor Guiliani, Al Qaeda, and the continuing threat of terrorist attack. A longer more descriptive "poem," the student felt, probably would not have had the richness this simple time reference has.

One of her classmates thought that while the metonymy the world has taken to heart and mind cannot represent the full horror of the day, "What more can we do? We communicate with signs and symbols all the time, and if we are careful, we are successful more often than not." I agree. Walker Percy pointedly observed that the deconstructionist is one who charges language with the inability to communicate but leaves a phone message for his wife to bring home a pepperoni pizza. If the critic's wife brings home the pizza requested, who can sincerely argue that language is "radically indeterminate." Isn't Derrida left with mozzarella in his mustache?

Does language ever fail us? Of course it does. Recall the postcard writer who wrote, "The scenery is here; wish you were beautiful." Or June Cleaver's famous command to her husband, "Ward, come upstairs and talk to the Beaver." Or this sign announcing the opening of a new business, "Owned and Operated by a Clemson Grad and Formal CU Football Player." Or this classified ad advertising a house for sale, "Brick, hardwood floors; this one won't last." Or this sentence from the *Fresno Bee*: "The new taxes will put debt-ridden Massachusetts back in the African-American." Or finally, George W. Bush saying on Oct. 18, 2004, "September the 4th, 2001, I stood in the ruins of the Twin Towers. It's a day I will never forget."

◌

To Derrida's claim that a text means nothing or so many things that it's meaningless, and to the fundamentalist's claim that a text has a single literal meaning, the New Critics might say as Laurence Perrine once argued, "A text may mean many things, not all of them." As an old New Critic, that places me squarely in the middle, which is where Aristotle said virtue resides. Postmodern theorists like Derrida have been described by their detractors as "gulls in a trawler's wake" or "eunuchs in a harem." Derrida's paragraph at the start of this essay is a long, unhappy way from John Crowe Ransom's definition, "[A critic is] one who in dealing with a work of art creates a little work of art in its honor."

Ransom's ideal is so lofty it makes me a bit dizzy, so my model is a bit more pragmatic: it's the work of a scholar like Dr. Matthew Bruccoli formerly of the University of South Carolina, one of whose specialties is American literature in the Jazz Age. I recall approaching him once when I was in graduate school about a problem I was having with a passage in *The Great Gatsby*. My question was whether the Montenegrin *Orderi de Danilo* medal that Gatsby claimed he was awarded in The Great War would have been inscribed in English. Professor Bruccoli smiled as he reached in his pocket and to my astonishment pulled out one of the rare Montenegrin medals he'd recently purchased at auction. He then pointed out that on his medal and all others like it there is no inscription because it is coated with a ceramic glaze that cannot be engraved. Now that's the sort of clarity and authority I expect from a critic!

For myself, I shall seek aid from critics and scholars of Bruccoli's caliber until Jacques Derrida and his disciples can give me definitive answers without brushing me off saying language and art can only approximate reality. We know that. And I shall abide by the words of Ernest Hemingway in *A Farewell to Arms*, "There were many words that you could not stand to hear and finally only the names of places had dignity. Certain numbers were the same way and certain dates and these with the names of places were all you could say and have them mean anything. Abstract words such as *glory, honor, courage,* or *hallow* were obscene beside the concrete names of villages, the numbers of roads, the names of rivers, the numbers of regiments and the dates." Did you hear that Professor Derrida? "Certain date...were all you could say and have them mean anything."

(A fuller version of this essay was published in *The Vocabula Review,* May 2006 and is available in the magazine's archives.)

Sacred Places and Spite Fences: Personal Space

"The mind is a meat marinated in place.
Each has a flavor absorbed from its base."
—The Wordspinner

"He and I had an office so tiny that an inch smaller and it would have been adultery."
—Dorothy Parker

Thanks to the US Army and its habit of moving soldiers every two or three years, I attended six grade schools and four high schools. As a consequence of my motility, I was slow to comprehend what Eudora Welty observed: "One place understood helps us understand all places better." As every botanist knows, plants with deep roots are more likely to survive the droughts and drafts nature imposes. Following twenty moves and the good luck to land a job in small university town, I promised myself I'd put down a taproot and ignore the fibrous laterals. Having lived in Clemson now for forty-four years (in the same house for thirty-two of them), I've come to believe that Welty was on to something since learning to appreciate how a template may be used to gauge the places beyond home.

For twenty-eight years, I felt like one of Arthur Schopenhauer's porcupines, moving closer for warmth in the winter, but yearning for some *Lebensraum* after being poked by the spines of a neighbor. However, despite my German heritage, I had no desire to invade Poland to get the space I felt entitled to. Today, in our split-level home of 2,300 square feet sitting on .6 of an acre, my wife and I seem to have found the right mix of propinquity and warmth. In other words, I don't want to go back to that seventh-floor Brooklyn apartment, nor do I have any desire to live so deeply in the woods that I cannot see the smoke rising from my neighbors' chimneys.

When we moved to Blue Ridge Drive with its view of the Appalachians to the west, we had a neighbor on our left flank whose idea of the Welcome Wagon was to build a five-foot board fence between us with the unfinished side facing out. He and his wife had lived on Blue Ridge undisturbed for many years and used the lot we bought as a yard-waste depository. Over twenty-five years, we spoke perhaps three or four times for a total of five minutes before he moved. By contrast, shortly after our house was built in 1980, a new house went up on our right flank. My wife baked some cookies, and together we went to greet the new neighbors. Ever since, they have mowed their grass well into our lot, and we mow ours well into theirs.

The art and science of proxemics is relatively new in human culture for the simple reason that humans living as hunter-gatherers were not territorial. No reason existed to mark one's territory when one rarely saw another human who wasn't family. Indeed, fifty thousand years ago, the world was one family's "oyster" with a circumference of 25,000 miles. As population densities increased, however, wild game, nuts, and berries started to run short, and before humans knew it, lines had been drawn in the sand and the sea: it's called the twelve-mile limit. An aerial limit also exists, but it's so poorly defined that Russian, Chinese, and US spy satellites orbit the Earth with impunity. That may end one day as others reach the high ground.

Animals, like countries, also have territorial limits. Each male grizzly occupies a circle that is about ten miles in diameter. Should his mate and her cubs happen to wander though, a father might well eat them. Should you wish to test the borders of the animal kingdom, hang glide near an eagle's nest, and you may find an angry bird tangled in your rigging trying to eat your liver. Or place two hundred and fifty wild Norway rats on a fenced-in, quarter-acre lot, and the creatures will turn into "hot little twitching death balls" despite an abundance of food. Tom Wolfe, however, was not describing rats when he wrote that memorable phrase; he was describing his fellow New Yorkers living in "O Rotten Gotham."

Indeed, humans have their own territorial needs, which vary with race, gender, national background, and criminal record. The distance between two conversing African-Americans averages tewnty-two inches; Caucasians, on the other hand, prefer five more inches to feel comfortable. Women stand closer to their girlfriends than men do; Arabs have no qualms about "getting up in your business" when they speak, and the volume of comfort zones for the incarcerated depends on the crime. Approach a violent criminal, and he'll tell you to stop three feet out, while nonviolent cons permit strangers to come within eighteen inches before they raise a hand.

Students of proxemics have observed that the more we "mark" our territory or regard a place as "ours," the more the "owners" are likely to defend it with strategies ranging from violence to passive aggression. Crime rates typically run much lower in two-story buildings than in taller complexes because residents feel less "at home" in the high-rises. Owners of automobiles with personalized license plates or customized sound systems are more likely to display symptoms of road rage because they perceive a passing car, for example, as an insult. And drivers leaving a parking place will typically exit in thirty-two seconds. However, if someone is waiting, the time increases to thirty-nine seconds. Should a waiting driver make the mistake of honking, the time grows to forty-three seconds.

Having ridden an elevator for forty-four years to an eighth-floor office,

I am something of a student of boxy mobile spaces. If an elevator leaves the first floor with eight people aboard, and two leave on the fourth floor, the six remaining passengers inevitably will shift locations to relieve the tension of their proximity by occupying the vacated space. Profundities like, "How about this hot weather?" may further ground some of the free electrons. But because of the brevity of the ride and the static electricity, it's rare when one hears a story on an elevator that one repeats at supper for the spouse. If it's "information spillover" you are looking for, you'll need a common area like a coffee lounge or a copier/printer room.

The online Khan Academy and Rosetta Stone programs may be fine for teaching the fundamentals of mathematics or language, but at some point in their development, students will always need face-to-face contact with likeminded peers and non-virtual teachers. For fifteen years, about 180 professors who shared Clemson's Strode Tower used a large coffee urn in the second-floor lounge of the nine-story building. When the urn died and the dean decided not to replace it, individuals started bringing hot plates to their offices to make coffee and tea. The lounge effectively died, and so did the cross-pollination that formerly occurred among members of the political science, music, nursing, foreign language, and English departments. I have several poems I can track directly to the old lounge while none is traceable to the workroom on the eighth floor. The death of the urn and the birth of email also had the effect of reducing what Steve Jobs tried to avoid at Pixar: the Rubik's cubicle-ization of workers.

One reason you probably have not heard of Bullfrog County, Nevada, is that it ceased to exist in 1989 when its population reached zero. As far as I know, nothing except some mineral wealth has ever come from this forsaken part of the planet where Yucca Mountain looms. If you want creativity, don't put people in elevators or cubicles, and don't ship them to Bullfrog County with your radioactive waste either. Instead, give them and Shakespeare's "sister" private offices with many opportunities to interact. I hate to think of the time when all universities resemble the University of Phoenix and Skyping replaces the seminar.

FROM RIVERS TO GLOCKENSPIELS: TIME AND CLOCKS

"Hour-glass man straddles the narrow orifice that is the present, unable to scale the future and fearful of spilling into the past."
—The Wordspinner

"If you can afford the blank-white face of Dior's diamond-studded watch, you can afford to be late."
—The Wordspinner

In the fall of 2011, I was trying to distinguish between temporal and eternal time for a class of freshmen. In Ron Rash's novel *Saints at the River,* Maggie, the narrator, says, "It suddenly seemed as if we had all gathered for this one moment. Except *moment* was the wrong word, because what I felt was an absence of the temporal, as if the mountains had shut us off not only from the rest of the world but from time." When a student asked what the author meant by "the temporal," I gestured toward the clock over the blackboard and said, "The temporal may be observed in the sweeping motion of our second hand. The minute and hour hands are also in motion, but unless you look very carefully, they appear eternally still as the Blue Ridge Mountains beyond our window. I wonder if Maggie realizes they once were 30,000 feet tall!"

"Uh, 'fessor," the student with temporal concerns said, "the second hand is hung up."

As I turned from the lectern while several of his classmates laughed, I realized that the second hand was just quivering in place, not advancing. "Well, then, I stand corrected," I said. "Time has stopped for this second hand but not the mountains."

Our concern for the present, which is no more than the correct time, is a fascinating human obsession. As a culture, we have invested millions in everything from pocket sundials to atomic clocks to determine the time when a second or minute either way really doesn't matter, does it? In the West, time is often understood as a river: a linear interpretation. In the East, time is a sea, ebbing and flooding: a cyclical interpretation. I prefer a blend of the two: something akin to the Upper Jordan's headwaters, which after a short run bulge forth in the Sea of Galilee. About ten miles south, the sea Jesus bestrode spills over a rocky ledge to form the Lower Jordan before washing into the Dead Sea, whose southern coast is the lowest point of dry land on the planet.

The sun then goes to work loosening the salt's grip, lifting moisture before dropping it on the greening hills north of Galilee. The beauty of this temporal figure is the suggestion of a pre-existence (the tributaries), an interim existence (the freshwater sea), and a post-existence (the river and the brine). For me, this "necessary fiction" makes richer sense of a difficult abstraction. Just as water is neither created nor destroyed in any large quantity on Earth, neither are the body's atoms, which are infinitely recycled through the multiverse.

American students of time are often surprised to learn that most household clocks as late as 1800 did not have a minute hand. Indeed the origin of "clock" (German *Glocke*, "bell") reminds us that the first mechanical timepieces had no hands at all: they were just a bell mechanism that chimed the canonical hour without a visual display. Thus time in a thirteenth-century monastery was better understood as regular aural events than a river or an arrow on a clock face. Just as the sundial and water clock had replaced timely observations of the moon and sun (Jews knew it was sundown when they could no longer distinguish between a red and black thread), so did the addition of the minute hand about 1275 define punctuality more narrowly for churchgoers and petitioners coming to city hall. Three hundred years later, the second hand was introduced, but few could afford one. At the start of the twentieth century, the best mechanical clocks were correct plus or minus one second over a year. By the 1930s, quartz-crystal technology improved precision to one second every five hundred years. In the near future, the atomic clock, which has been proposed for the International Space Station, should lose or gain a second every 313 million years, but what chronometer could you check it against? Like I said, it's an odd obsession we humans have, but if we are ever going to navigate among the stars, accuracy to the trillionth of a second will be essential.

I once facetiously proposed a clock of my own design: a giant *campanile* to be set on a hummock in Kansas with chimes loud enough to be heard by everyone in the "lower forty-eight." I argued that such a clock would put us all in the same time zone and end the nonsense of allowing my sister in Arizona to ignore daylight savings time, but a friend observed that given the relatively slow rate at which sound travels, the East and West coast would still not be synchronized with Chicago and Topeka.

"Clock designers" like myself have often been dreamers. Over the last millennium, the world has used scent clocks (a different smell for each hour), spice clocks (a different taste for each hour), touch watches for the blind, a cuckoo wrist watch, clocks inside silver skulls displaying the time remaining before the owner's death, Jewish clocks that run counterclockwise, and Muslim clocks that point to Mecca and sound an alarm for each appointment with the prayer rug. For the Romantic, there's the Movado "museum watch" without any numbers; for the Classicist, there's a dial with Roman numerals and thirty-three functions. Since I rarely need to know when the moon is going to set over Java, I prefer an analog watch with a clean face and a sweep-second hand for timing a grandson in the forty-yard dash.

To illustrate how clocks can manipulate the time they tell, nothing beats the old "mill clock." These Satanic devices, reportedly used in textile mills in the US and Great Britain, ran slow during work time and rapidly during lunch breaks. Workers were forbidden to bring watches of their own to work.

The house and garage my wife and I own has thirty-five time pieces making springing forward and falling back a semi-annual nightmare. Why so many? Try buying a car, radio, TV, or computer without one. Given the frequency with which we see the time displayed, no wonder "time" is the most often used noun in English. But as an analog man in a digital age, I long for a return to a time when it was less visible, more flexible, and I didn't feel like Harold Lloyd hanging from an hour hand several stories above the street. I am *not* thinking of the alarm clock a nephew of mine devised when he had a paper route requiring him to rise at four in the morning. Every night, he set his alarm and opened his window. When the alarm went off in the attic bedroom of his Maplewood, New Jersey home, the light-sleeping neighbors telephoned my sister who then went upstairs to wake her son. Instead, I prefer my Seiko that seismic activity, I've been assured, will rewind in the grave.

The First Drafts of Myth: Anecdotes

"We must restore to poetry the force of narrative."
—James Dickey

"Abstractions are best understood in a story."
—Anonymous

The deeper I sally into my "anecdotage," as H. L. Mencken called the chatty age, the more concerned I am when I see two college students in a restaurant "building communities," twittering on their cell phones with invisible parties while ignoring each other. Or three friends headed to the gym, each rolling to a different beat emanating from their iPods. Is the oral tradition in its death throes? I trust not, for I have many tales left to tell, but what's a tale to a self-absorbed audience?

I credit my old mentor James Dickey with convincing me that the best teaching is anecdotal. He told a rapt class that when *Deliverance* was filmed, the corpse that Dickey as the sheriff unveiled was not the actor playing Drew, as he had expected, but Christopher his son. Surprise! For years when I taught the novel, I told this and other Dickey-ian tales, and I sensed that they lent my comments an intimacy and *gravitas* they might not otherwise have enjoyed.

Dickey was hard to follow, but eventually I understood what he'd been trying to dramatize for his classes. Early in my teaching career, I remember rattling on to a class of sophomores about Alexander Pope's rococo masterpiece *The Rape of the Lock*. I looked up from my lecture notes and saw two students sleeping and the rest staring at snow drifting across the campus. I quietly elbowed my Norton anthology off the lectern to wake the sleepers, and said, "What the Baron does to Belinda is a bit like the time I got drunk in the army." The few heads not turned my way after Norton hit the floor now snapped to attention. "I went home from the Florida Bar with a woman named Doris, had a schnapps, and fell asleep in an easy chair. Little did I know that Doris's sister Babs lived in the apartment as well, for this was the first and last time I was ever there."

"Sure it was," muttered a youthful cynic.

"When I awoke," I continued, trying to ignoring the titters, "both women were giggling over me, one with a razor in hand, the other with a bowl of water and a towel. When I asked what the joke was, Doris handed me a mirror. One look and I realized that I no longer had a unibrow." I told the suddenly interested class that I understood how violated Belinda had felt, for no one wants his or her appearance altered without their consent.

Belinda stormed off to the Cave of Spleen, and I slunk back to the barracks with my hat pulled down low.

The interjection of self into a classroom presentation virtually assures attention will be paid, but nothing can guarantee quality. However, one test of a good story is how often it is misappropriated. My old friend Harold Woodell, a gifted storyteller, found the perfect place to insert the bittersweet tale of his mother's stroke in an American Humor class. It seems that his mother blacked out as she was driving in an urban-industrial area and ended up wedging her car between two telephone poles, leaving it, he added, "like a tube of toothpaste squeezed at one end." When she came to, bruised and embarrassed, a cameraman was shooting through a broken windshield, and a television reporter was thrusting a microphone in her face, asking her how the accident happened. In words inappropriate for the news at eleven or any other time of day, she told the reporter where she could file her microphone. As Harold was winding up his tale, a student said, "That was Dr. Smith's mother!"

"It was not!" exclaimed my colleague, "I have pictures of the accident we took for the insurance adjustor." After searching his memory banks, Harold realized he had told the story in the faculty lounge when Dr. Smith was present. Smith then appropriated the tale and told it slightly modified in classes of his own. Apparently he'd been dining out on the story's strength for years. Perhaps Smith "winked" and the student missed it, or he'd told it so often, he convinced himself it was his own.

Speaking of the storyteller's wink, the Arabs start a fairy tale recitation, "There was, there was not." This provides the teller a convenient escape route, not inherent in "once upon a time," should the audience question the truth of the tale. The last time we hired an arborist, I started my usual round of questions, probing for a story. "Squirrel," as this patched-eye, pulpwood cutter had been dubbed, was well known in the greater Pickens County area for his tall tales. As we chatted over the hood of his old pickup while his two sons went to work on a dead pine, a red-tailed hawk appeared, wheeling and screeching between us and a pale moon. Immediately Squirrel whistled back, and the two began a shrill dialogue that lasted a couple of minutes. When I managed to get his attention again, I said that it appeared the hawk recognized Squirrel.

"I saved his life a couple of years ago," he said. "He was diving after a rabbit when he smashed into the grill of my truck. I stopped and pulled him free before driving to the vet. She patched him up, and my wife and I fed him raw hamburger for a few weeks. Ever since, he has followed me to every job I've worked. Hawks are loners with a taste for warm blood, but they never forget a favor."

Maybe it happened, maybe not, but what Squirrel said next had the imprimatur of Bishop Truth.

As the hawk sailed off, I asked him how he'd lost the vision in one eye. He said his crew had been taking down some trees for a contractor while he did what he did best, supervise. His sons were grinding tree limbs beside an office complex under construction. Suddenly and violently, their father was struck in the face by a flying object of unknown origin. One of the sons called an ambulance, and in less than thirty minutes, Squirrel was in the OR at Oconee Memorial Hospital. Everyone assumed that something had been kicked back from the limb grinder, but the surgeon discovered a twelve-penny nail lodged across the cheekbone and eyebrow, which accounted for the vertical facial scars before me. Had the projectile, which came from a nail gun at the construction site, been turned at any other angle, it would have flown through the eye and into his brain.

Oral tales lose so much in transcription that I wonder sometimes why I bother to write them down. My best answer is that despite recent technological threats to face-to-face conversation and storytelling, we are at heart a narrative species just as chimps are groomers and dolphins love to play. Instinctively, we all want to know, "What happened next?" or, "How did it turn out?" Often the verisimilitude of a tale is immaterial because each, modified to suit the teller, has its own truth. Most events in our lives do not have a neat beginning, middle, and end, but we all have a right to structure the record to express the point we wish to make. Utilizing "the creative possibilities of the lie," as James Dickey called it, often is the difference between a riff and a melody.

EARLY DON'T LAST LONG: CARPE DIEM

"If you've got a frog to swallow, don't study it too long."
—Anonymous

"Too soon the future is yesterday,
and still we sleep most of Saturday."
—The Wordspinner

Have you ever been in a movie theater when suddenly the sound becomes distorted or the focus grows fuzzy? Well, I'm the guy in the aisle seat near the back who finally gets up and goes to find the manager. "*Carpe diem et noctem*" (seize the day and the night) has long been a motto of those who grew up as I did with a Presbyterian conscience. As my Sunday school teacher in South Georgia used to say, "If you ain't doin', you ain't deservin'."

One form of "doin'" that I enjoy is observing how many ways a chestnut can be pulled from the fire. I've been rescuing the Roman poet Horace's "carpe diem" ever since high school Latin, and I'm nowhere near shutting down that service.

Let's start with the carpe punsters: there's the antiquarian book dealer whose business is Carpe Libris, the extroverted poet who confesses that he loves to "carpe the podium," the jealous feminist aiming to "carpe every swinging testicle," the allusive angler who urges us to "seize the carp," the psychiatrist who advises her patients to "carpe your demons and throttle them," and the dog breeder who begs us to "Shar-Pei diem" or "seize the wrinkled dog."

Then there are the spinoffs that start from "seize." In 2005, the state of Maryland's Department of Tourism adopted the slogan, "Seize the day off." A consumer magazine for people with allergies and asthma calls itself Sneezetheday. More than one student has told me that Horace wrote, "Cease the day." And in 2008, some anonymous classics majors picketed the University of London, which was threatening to make cuts in their program, with signs reading, "Caesar the day." Come to think of it, "Caesar the day" could be a salad packaged for takeout, but it isn't—yet.

As a former literature and humanities teacher, I passed hardly a week without deconstructing the carpe theme in one author or another from "Let us eat and drink for tomorrow we shall die" in Isaiah, to "What is love? 'Tis not hereafter," in Shakespeare, to "Gather ye rosebuds while ye may" in Robert Herrick, to "Do not hurry, do not rest" in Goethe, to "Let us endeavor to live so that when we come to die even the undertaker will be sorry" in Mark Twain, to "Rage, rage against the dying of the light" in Dylan Thomas, to "There never was a body give an undertaker a tip" in Flannery O'Connor, and, to "If the doctor told me I had five minutes to live, I'd type faster" in Isaac Asimov.

Hearing their teachers harp on this notion as often as they do, students have developed their own versions of the ubiquitous theme. One golfer told me to "putt while the irons are hot" as a way to stop over thinking my softball game. A fan of the psychedelic guitarist Jerry Garcia of the Grateful Dead said he was taking his spring break on the road where he hoped to "eat, drink, and see Jerry." Wishing he could join him, his roommate advised, "Boogie 'til you puke, dude."

Like students, teachers have their own variations on the theme. In the 1980s, Lee Morrissey, a former colleague who was educated in the Boston area, moved to New York.

In class one day at Columbia (à la Robin Williams as Mr. Keating), Morrissey urged his students to "capé the day."

A puzzled student asked if he meant "carpe."

"No," the instructor insisted, "it's capé; that's the way all my teachers in Boston said it." He later apologized.

I'm sure I've never read a complete management book, but from the office posters I've seen, business gurus must have taken Horace to heart. In the marketing department of a large Charlotte bank, I saw employees being urged to "Get all the wood behind one arrowhead." Judging from another poster, the boss apparently liked to be reminded to "have lunch or be lunch." I have not seen it on a poster yet, but I know one business professor who liked to tell people on the university curriculum committee, "To ask permission is to seek denial." Finally, Cosmo Kramer, the "hipster doofus" of Seinfeld television fame, often had a hard time managing his own life, but he sounded positively managerial when he concluded a telephone order for a Chinese meal with, "extra MSG."

Speaking of aggressive managers and marketing, Nike's "Just do it" campaign has been very successful just as "Go for the gusto" has worked for Schlitz, and "Life is short, play hard" has worked for Reebok. Not wishing to be left in the dust of all those sneakered beer drinkers, the National Federation of Colombian Coffee Growers has urged people since the 1990s to "grab life by the beans." I can only speak for myself, but this line always makes me clench my butt and draw my knees in.

Once after Juan Valdez had finished telling me that coffee grown in the mountains is richer than that grown in the valleys, Tim McGraw's country hit, "Live like You Were Dying" came on the radio. Had that been followed by an ad for *The Dead Poets Society*, I would have quit my yoga class and dropped all pretense of reflection.

Coincidences aside, the comic pages of the *Greenville News* have supplied me with some of my favorite efflorescences of the carpe theme. After a rare day in which everything went his way, Jeremy of Zits told his closest friend, "I totally carped the snot out of this diem." It appears that the Zits creators, Jerry Scott and Jim Borgman, may have been recycling one of the most memorable Calvin and Hobbes appearances. As Calvin undresses preparing to bathe one evening, he tells his stuffed tiger, "My elbows are grass-stained, I've got sticks in my hair, I'm covered in bug bites and scratches. I've got sand in my socks and leaves in my shirt, my hands are sticky with sap, and my shoes are soaked! I'm hot, dirty, itchy, and tired." Leaning against the tub, a smiling Hobbes says, "I say consider this day seized!"

Lest you think that I've been mocking Horace, let me close with an analogy to what my predecessor more succinctly observed two thousand years ago.

Every day is a matchstick. You wake in the dark and strike the business end of a match against its box containing a finite but unknown number of tomorrows. If you have struck it with the right speed and pressure, it flares up before slowly burning down to anxious fingertips. Meanwhile, two fingers of the other hand drop the box and go to the mouth for some saliva. Then gently grasping the curling black stem, you wait as spit sizzles harmlessly in the index-thumb gap. Slowly the match is turned upside down while you shield the flame from a stray breeze with cupped hands. Once the flame has died and the stick cooled, it is pulverized and placed in the compost. Only now, do you sit back and contemplate the dispersal of a day's light that has been seized.

EIGHT LIVES AND COUNTING: CURIOSITY

"Too much curiosity lost paradise."
—Aphra Behn

"The world will not perish for want of wonders, but for want of wonder."
—J. B. S. Haldane

In *Smart Questions to Ask about Your Children's Education*, Dorothy Leeds ruefully reports that American four-yearolds ask more questions than college students—on average, three hundred each day for the kindergartners, twenty for their elders. As a grandfather of four and a teacher of more than four thousand stdents over the last forty-two years, I suspect Leeds is correct. About the only way I get questions from my students is to require one per class in writing on the day's reading assignment. I admit I get some pretty lame questions ("How much do you think Shakespeare got for this story?"), but I also receive a handful that make me rethink something I've been teaching for thirty years or more.

I was fortunate in some respects—I flunked out of Georgia Tech after one quarter, enlisted in the Army for three and a half years, learned a trade, and took a front-row seat before the Iron Curtain to hone my craft. When I returned to the classroom, I had read some books, seen some opera, tasted dark beer, married the love of my life, and was a different student altogether. If reading and traveling had dampened my sponge, my German wife was shaming me to act responsibly, so I was eager to absorb just about anything my instructors proposed and the curriculum demanded.

Another thing going for me is the pure chance event that I was born before 1955. That's the year childhood changed according to Howard Chudacoff, a cultural historian at Brown University. The mid-to late fifties, Chudacoff notes, is when *The Mickey Mouse Club* debuted on television, and toy manufacturers began shilling their wares year round instead of three weeks before Christmas. Lego kits and the like with explicit instructions instead of wooden blocks and marbles, he argues, began limiting imaginative play.

This subtle change has led to a decline in "executive function skills," which is his way of saying today's children are not as self-controlled and independent as their grandparent's generation. Last fall while playing whiffle ball with two kids in the neighborhood, I said, "OK, Tommy, go back to the plate, and hit again; there's an imaginary man on first." He looked at me as if I'd said, "Imagine your name is Darth." A fly-faced alien could wake this lad with a golden antenna bobbing from its exposed cerebellum, and he wouldn't think to ask whence it came.

Along the same lines, there is the cautionary tale of my former student, Zoneeki Scott. (I've changed his name, but not by much, to protect myself from Scott's lawyers.) On the first day of class, I was reading the roll when I came to Scott's name, and I was so sure the computer had made a mistake I said, "Scott Zoneeki?"

"Here, sir, but you have it backwards. My name is Zoneeki Scott."

"Your first name is Zoneeki?"

"Yes, sir."

"Interesting. I'm quite sure I've never heard your name before—how did you come by such an unusual name?"

"I don't know."

"You don't know."

"No, sir."

"Are there any uncles or grandfathers in your family named Zoneeki?"

"No, sir, not that I know of."

"Do you have any brothers or sisters?"

"Yes, sir."

"What are their names if you don't mind my asking?"

"William and Maryanne."

"William, Maryanne, and Zoneeki—and you never asked."

"No, sir."

"What a shame. Be sure to ask next time you call home, OK?" And that was the end of it. Mr. Scott dropped the class shortly after the first quiz but before he had a chance to satisfy my idle curiosity.

If Zoneeki represents the impotence of the imagination, what stands for success? I've long admired the anonymous non-com who caused Gen. Eisenhower to chuckle. Ike and his men were on pre-war maneuvers, and after "Red Army" sappers had "exploded" a Louisiana bridge, they placed a "DESTROYED" sign on it. Later, Ike observed elements of the "Blue Army" crossing this bridge. "Sergeant," yelled Ike, "Can't you see that bridge is down?"

"With all due respect, sir, we're swimming."

Thomas Friedman has written that America's future depends on 100,000 home workshops and the innovative work done therein to create the next Hewlett-Packard or Microsoft. A great deal is riding on America's successor to Bill Hewlett, Dave Packard, and Bill Gates, but if the ever-green forest of our nation's youth has been defoliated by toys that stultify instead of stimulate, what is to become of us? As Eric Sevareid once wrote, "It is not the hardening of the arteries I fear but the hardening of the imagination."

Computer games, television, and Lego kits aren't the only culprits here; I blame the fundamentalist church as well. I've taught my share of "the frozen chosen," and I've yet to meet one with a fully thawed imagination. The church, of course, has dampened the intellectual enthusiasm of children for centuries especially among its women, for Eve more than Adam, the church has argued, is responsible for our unfortunate fall. Picking up the cue like the good apostle he is, Luke warns us to remember the salty fate of Lot's wife, that curious woman who could not bear to leave home without a backward glance. And St. Augustine pronounced curiosity a "disease." Of course, we've all stuck our noses in places we shouldn't have, but unless a few of our kind are willing to create some ferment occasionally, there is no Chardonnay, and we are left with a saccharine syrup that rots our teeth.

Let me close with a slightly more extended tale starring the imagination. In 1945, Arthur C. Clarke wrote a fanciful yet pragmatic letter to the editor of *Wireless World* in which he proposed using German-style V-2 rockets to place geosynchronous communication satellites in orbit. No one including Einstein, who thought imagination was more important than knowledge, had ever dreamed of such a thing. Twenty years later, Intelsat 1 began circling the planet like a carpenter bee around an unpainted fascia board. In 2009, there are close to four hundred communication satellites in "Clarke orbits" some 22,000 miles overhead.

So it seems to this observer that unless our collective brain is regularly willing to raise its periscope, how will we know who wrote the Book of Love, what is one to make of a diminished thing, can we afford to stand idly by, does an increase in knowledge necessarily mean an increase in sorrow, and does He smile His work to see?

Running Out of Sheepgoats: Excuses

"Humans always need an n-word."
—The Wordspinner

"It is important to run out of scapegoats."
—Sheldon Kopp

In the Dubya era, I recall overhearing my German wife say that Alberto Gonzalez, Bush's attorney general, was being used as a "sheepgoat" in the waterboarding scandal. Her fellow expatriate did not indicate whether he caught that slip of the tongue, so I kept my mouth shut. When the time was right, I said, "Oh, by the way, sheep have nothing to do with scapegoats. It was a *goat* that assumed the sins of the people before *escaping* into the Judean wilderness."

"I thought it was a sheep," Ingrid said. "That's my excuse."

"No, that's your reason," I said. "You don't need an excuse."

"What's the difference?"

"Well, if a student lied telling me a paper was late because her computer had a virus, that would be an excuse. If she was telling the truth, that would be her reason."

Sorting the truth from the untruth, of course, is a delicate undertaking, and until we have an app for lying on our iPads, it will remain a close call. I remember a class in which eight of the thirty missed a major examination. Seven confessed they were unprepared and took a letter-grade reduction; the eighth said her grandmother had died, and she'd gone home for the funeral. Without emailing or phoning me, she just skipped town with the oldest excuse in the book. How common is it? One colleague had students sign the following statement, "The undersigned grants that all his/her grandparents are dead or in good health." Of course, he soon discovered that requirement didn't stop the grim reaper from harvesting some aunts and uncles before test time. My own red-eyed student brought me the obituary I had requested, slapped it on my desk, and said she resented the implication that she was lying. I said I had eight absentees and asked her how she would have handled the matter. "I would have trusted me," she said. She had a point: she had a low A average, had taken fewer than the allowable cuts, and had turned in all of her assignments on time, so I let her make up the test without any deductions. As Duke University learned from the rape accusations against members of its lacrosse team, nothing is black and white.

One reason that excuses interest me is their universality; they appear to be a common human denominator. When Hurricane Katrina swept over New Orleans in 2005, "meteorologist" Pat Robertson discovered what he claimed was the cause of the record low-pressure system in the town's gay bars. A year earlier when a tsunami rolled across the Indian Ocean, Indonesian mullahs of a geological bent accused women who did not cover their heads of causing the devastation in Aceh. Once cross-eyed children were blamed for crop failures, but as the world has shrunk and western styles have spread east, the guilt has shifted. On the other hand, in the west, women who wear an Eastern-style head scarf are asking for trouble. Who knew that hair was such a mischief-maker?

Another reason I collect excuses is their accidental humor. Take those written by parents for their children: "Please excuse Mary who is administrating," or Tom, "who has an acre in his side," or Dick, "who has loose vowels," or Jane, "who is in bed with gramps." No dead grandmothers, just "an overactive stigmata."

The comic visual artist does not have to travel far for inspiration. Who can forget the Zambian tennis player who said he lost a match because his jockstrap was too tight and his opponent farted with every serve? Or the Chicago Bulls' general manager who found the "inexperience of the building" to have been a factor in the team's losses? Or the Vice President who claimed TV's *Murphy Brown* caused the Los Angeles riots? Or the Soviet hockey coach who pinned the team's Olympic loss on a "shortage of hockey sticks"? Blessed are hockey sticks and sitcoms, for they make great scapegoats and stories.

Often a legitimate excuse morphs into a mental block. Jim, an artist friend, found that he could not paint knowing there was a leak in the skylight of his studio. Though the crack was small and the work below was protected, just knowing his "sanctuary" had this flaw left Jim artistically impotent for six months. Some might say Jim simply didn't want to work, but having suffered from writer's block, I know how everything from global warming to the mercury in my fillings can keep me from my keyboard.

For some things, there is simply no excuse. When Pratt-Whitney charged the Pentagon $999 for a pair of pliers, the fact that the tool "installed a clip as well as removed it" was no reason for the egregious overcharge. When former Senator John Edwards justified his adultery by saying his wife was "in remission from breast cancer," that was unacceptable on any level. And when Adolf Eichmann justified the murder of eleven million innocents because he and other pawns like him had received orders from a man they regarded as God's vicar, no court on Earth with the possible exception of the Spanish Inquisition would acquit them.

Given the right excuse, a human is seemingly capable of anything. With the Russians already travelling the subways of Berlin in April of 1945, Mrs. Magda Goebbels told an aide that National Socialism meant so much to her that she would not be evacuated from the capital and dishonor her government's cause. Moreover, she felt certain her children agreed. "Certainly my reason tells me," she said, "that I can't leave them to…the Jewish revenge." With that uncertain fate in mind, she poisoned all six of them, the oldest being twelve.

The technicality, which is legally correct but immoral, may be the worst excuse of all. In 2011 when a tornado flattened Joplin, Missouri, nurse Mark Lindquist did all he could to save three lives in his charge. Unfortunately the three died and Lindquist was injured so badly, he was in a coma for two months and accumulated $2.5 million in medical expenses. His insurance company denied his claim saying he was at "no greater risk than the general public at the time…" Apparently, if everybody is injured, it's just another day at the office.

Be careful, gentle reader, of the finely engraved excuses in the boilerplate.

ALL ENGINE AND NO BRAKE? FREE SPEECH

"Congress shall make no law...abridging the freedom of speech..."
—James Madison

"It is the absolute right of the state to supervise the formulation of public opinion."
—Josef Göbbels

Several years ago in a *Greenville News* guest editorial, a friend and former colleague retoasted the old chestnut about falsely shouting fire in a crowded theater. I wrote him privately and teasingly reminded him of a scene in Aristophanes' comic masterpiece *Lysistrata* in which the old men of Athens build a "fire" on stage to smoke out the women who have seized the Acropolis where the city's treasury is located. I said that if one of these old men shouts "Fire!" he is well within his rights whether the fire is real or not. It's in the script. But if the director shouts "Fire" from back stage or the mezzanine, and there's a panic, he's subject to penalties. My point is that there are limits to what, where, when, and how we speak off stage.

The First Amendment's forty-five words have not been revised since they were written in 1791. Numerous court decisions since then, however, have effectively truncated what many Americans still consider a constitutional guarantee of absolute free speech. But absolutes are best left in the physics lab where the speed of light has been exceeded, and absolute zero has been approached to within one tenth of a billionth of a degree Kelvin. The heirs of Einstein have precious few absolutes left, moral or otherwise.

Despite the Supreme Court's truncations, many academics in 2012 still regard the freedom to speak in a classroom as unconditional. Forty years ago, I probably felt the same way; today, I have reservations. These may have begun when I glossed a scene in a humanities class involving Homer's treatment of Ganymede and Zeus. I said the fictional relationship was pedophilic and left it at that, but what if I'd earnestly advocated child rape from my bully pulpit? A more experienced colleague said that I might well champion such a position, but there's nothing in any tenure contract that stops a university from firing me for what it considers moral turpitude. I don't think I could blame them.

By the same token, should a chemistry professor in the name of relevance teach students to cook crystal meth in a freshman lab? Does a physics teacher have the right to demonstrate to undergraduates how to make a nuclear device if one can gather enough radium from old clock faces?

Does a microbiology professor have the right to show sophomores how to cultivate anthrax spores? Can a college football coach at the Air Force Academy hang a banner in the dressing room reading, "I am a member of Team Jesus Christ first"? Or do elementary school teachers have the right to teach prejudice?

In Riceville, Iowa at the height of the civil rights movement, a third-grade teacher decided that she would teach her pupils about racial prejudice. She, therefore, told her all-white class that brown-eyed children are superior to blue. Within minutes, the tenor of the class changed. The following day, she told her charges she'd been mistaken: blue-eyed children are superior. In short order, the blues were pushing the browns off the sliding boards at recess. An unannounced stunt like that today would get a teacher fired; in the sixties, she was interviewed like a celebrity though many in the state regarded her as "evil."

I'll never forget the self-professed neo-Nazi I taught in a sophomore American literature course. During a discussion of Phillis Wheatley, the young skinhead expressed his view that without the poet's white owners and patrons, she never would have set pen to paper. In the class discussion of Frederick Douglass, he said the black abolitionist would not have become a writer without the white genes of his former owner and father. I wanted to wring his pimply neck, but I cornered my tongue and let the class put him in his place. Some of my best classroom moments have involved saying nothing while the free speech of my students won the day.

But let's leave the classroom and pursue the issue of speech limits elsewhere. Should angry disabled vets be permitted to burn a flag at Arlington? No, but I'd support them if they burned one in their front yard after being denied VA compensation they felt they were entitled to. Should a Muslim woman living in the US be allowed to pose for her driver's license picture with only her eyes showing behind her veil? For reasons of public safety in this age of terrorism, she may not, but she can wear her burka in the grocery, on the beach, and in the bowling alley if she wishes. Does anyone have the right to preach on Main Street using a megaphone? No, but I'd support their right to speak if they'd take their sermons to the Speakers' Corner of the local Hyde Park. They need to lose the megaphone too if houses or businesses are near. Do teachers of minority literature have a right to invite members of the KKK to their classrooms? No, but I'd support them if they arranged the talk for a campus auditorium where the police could insure the safety of all. Do Muslim prayer calls have a right to drift into Roman Catholic neighborhoods? I think so because the tolling of Catholic bells in Muslim neighborhoods violates no noise ordinances. Should the Rev. Fred Phelps be permitted to denounce the friends of a homosexual Marine at his funeral? Of course not, but I'd support Phelps's right to speak against homosexuals in the military in a public forum. Should an interviewer be permitted to change a quotation as long as the meaning is not substantially altered? In my opinion, quotation marks are sacred, but the courts now permit changes. Should a farmer be allowed to make a rope noose to help him haul hay bales into his hayloft? Of course, but he may not hang this noose from a tree in his black neighbor's yard. And finally, just as no one had the right to publish Anne Frank's address in 1942, diplomatic cables that hide no crime, trade secrets, patient records, student transcripts, nuclear encryption codes, wartime troop movements, and the identity of undercover police are all restricted "speech."

Jet-powered automobiles more suitable for the Bonneville Salt Flats should be banned from public highways for the same reason that one person's absolute liberty threatens the rest of us. Freedom, as my father likes to say, is a lot like salt—a pinch sharpens the flavor, but a pound will kill you.

From Handshakes to Fist Bumps: Departures

"Safe home."
—Anonymous

"Eclipse yourself."
—Anonymous

Years ago when the editor-in-chief of *Weekly Hubris* was teaching journalism at Clemson University, I chanced upon her waiting for an elevator in Strode Tower.

"Waiting for Godot?" I asked.
"No," she replied, "a streetcar named Desire."
Unable to follow that reply at the level it deserved, I took the steps to my office. I might have said, "Go, and catch a falling star," or, "Wherever you go, there you are," or, "Go where glory awaits you," but I took the stairs less traveled by.

Threshold rituals surely originated when hunter-gatherers met each other on the East African savannah where thresholds may have been defined by the last place someone urinated. Freud argued that civilization began when someone cast a word instead of a stone at a stranger. Since that word probably was a threat, I'd argue that it began when we learned to say, "You are well come."

Since then, greetings have fluttered between these high and low poles: "All's well, and the goose hangs high," to, "Gimme some hungry chicken," while departures have fluctuated between, "Go, tribe, and hark upon the gale," to, "Let's make like the sheep and get the flock out." In between, lie hundreds of variations such as, "Howdy," "Daddy's home, release the doves," "Plutardo," "Tata for now," "Keep your skillet greased," "Hello, brother of another mother," "Good morning, damn you," and, "May the wattle fairy never darken your door."

Perhaps the most cordial greeting ever extended to me by a stranger came from Bishop Desmond Tutu. My wife and I were attending the graduation ceremonies of our son and daughter at the University of South Carolina, and to our great surprise and pleasure, Bishop Tutu was the keynote speaker. After the school president introduced him, the bishop stepped to the lectern and said to the hushed crowd of perhaps ten thousand, "The God in me greets the God in you." Whatever tension caused by a black man addressing a mostly white audience in a red state was instantly dispelled. The bishop, I believe, would agree that polite hellos and goodbyes are a lot like sacraments: outward and audible signs of an inner and spiritual grace.

After the ceremonies, I presumptuously and probably superfluously added a line of my own to Tutu's greeting:

"Whether you're Christian, Muslim, or Jew,
The God in me greets the God in you."

Later, when I mentioned Tutu's greeting in class, an Indian exchange student informed me that the South African was simply but elegantly translating the Sanskrit Namaste, which means, "I bow to the divine in you," or, "I honor your spirit," both of which harken to the ecumenical ideal admired by religious progressives the world over.

When contemporary cartoonists set a scene at a threshold, they generally exploit the awkwardness of the unexpected. As Tom Wilson's Ziggy enters an IRS office, he is met by a sign that says, "Assume the position," and thinks, "Whatever happened to 'Please take a seat'?" As David Sipress's urban couple approaches another pair, the husband whispers to his wife, "Quick! Remind me—are they handshakers, [or] huggers...?" And as two dogs drawn by Peter Steiner sniff each other's anuses, one says, "What say we find another way to say hello?" Cartoon departures likewise are characterized by an assortment of emotions. One half of Gahan Wilson's amoeba in the process of splitting says to his better half, "I suppose this is goodbye." Sometimes partings are indignant as when David Reilly's woman on her cell phone says, "I'm coming to a tunnel, so goodbye and go to hell." And the rhyming farewell has never been quite as light as Charles Schultz's, "Toodle-oo, Caribou! In a while, Crocodile! Stay loose, Mongoose! It's been neat, Parakeet!"

Perhaps seeking some relief from the Depression and the war, American rimesters made playful greetings popular in the 1930s and 40s. "Hello, Joe, what do you know?" "What's cookin', good lookin'?" and, "What's knittin', kitten?" were, according to my recently deceased mother, commonplace. Punning greetings like, "Hi, gossip, what's the news?" "Hi, sprout, what's growin'?" and, "Hi, Sugar, are you rationed?" likewise were all the rage in the Big Band era, and few riveting Rosies took offense. After a long day of riveting, who can blame them?

The playfully interactive greeting has, I suppose, always been popular with children. I once was asked to speak to a fourth-grade class about the origins of personal names including the students' own. The class was excited by the promise of a stranger, and I didn't help matters when I went up to several of them and said, "Gimme some hungry chicken." A student of mine had recently taught me this variation on the old "Give me five" routine. As I entered the classroom, it occurred to me that something new and fun would help gain the class's respect. Of course, I had to explain that when I said, "Gimme some hungry chicken" the person being greeted should extend an open hand. It was from this that the "chicken" would hungrily "peck" the proffered "grain." Unfortunately for the class's teacher, the kids continued their pecking long after I left.

Departures are often characterized by a bit of romantic "glue," which communicates, "Despite my absence, I'm still stuck on you." Though my German wife and I are MOPs, married old people, we still feel the need to squeeze out some mucilage as we go our separate ways. After I kiss her goodbye, I say "Juice" (an Anglicized variation on tschüs or "bye"), and she says, "Luba du" or "Lova du" (Anglicized forms of "Ich liebe dich," or, "I love you"). I then say "See-ox" (because in German "Sioux" is pronounced "see-ox" which sounds a bit like "see you"), and she goes to the window to wave as I back out of the driveway flashing my "light horn." Elements of the sentimental routine come and go, but in one form or another, it has served an adhesive purpose for almost fifty years. On my return or hers, the reception is not quite as elaborate but every bit as ceremonious. I suppose we just don't have the energy, or it's obvious the "glue" has held.

Speaking of personalized farewells, my friend Dr. Jim Skinner of Presbyterian College fondly relates his mother's habit of asking her children whenever they left the house, "Do you have a handkerchief?" Initially, this ritual was a helpful reminder, but it soon became annoying before eventually turning into an endearing trademark. Jim and his three brothers finally reached the point that when they heard the question, they would simply pull their hankies from their back pockets and wave them without so much as a backward glance as if to say with a sigh, "Yes, Mother, I have my handkerchief." When she died a few years ago, the four men concluded the funeral service by pulling out their handkerchiefs and waving them eloquently over the casket.

William James thought habitual ceremonies were "the flywheel of society...its precious [momentum-conserving] agent." Others have regarded them as the rocky ballast in the ship's hold, which in a storm is worth its weight in platinum. I could not agree more, for whatever the metaphor, the brevity of these rituals belies their steely, stony weight.

Plays on Words

Because a Thousand Trillion Synapses Aren't Enough: The Card File

"Great things are not done by impulse, but by a series of small things brought together."
—Vincent Van Gogh

"Skip likes the quare thing that snaps the routine—
in one appendix, a sprouting bean."
—The Wordspinner

I began filing in self-defense. Mother accused me of forgetting to send her a birthday present, but my wife and I knew we had sent her something—we just couldn't recall what it was. Suddenly we both felt like the farmer standing in the pasture with a rope in his hand, not sure if he'd found the rope or lost the cow. A few years earlier, I'd started filing classroom materials in manila folders after a professor of mine at Auburn said he summarized the contents of every academic article he read on one or more three-by-five cards. When I went to see him, I noticed that in a corner of his office was a small card catalogue. I was tempted to break in just to see how he had it all organized, for it was one thing to file something but another to find it. A decade passed before I understood the virtue of the card system.

My dealings with Mother were simplified once I started the "Mother" file folder. A record of anything she or Dad sent or I sent them went into the file. Showing the preliminary symptoms of dementia a few years later, she claimed she had bought us a car, which I knew was incorrect, but Dad's memory was merely porous, unlike Mother's, which was porous and creative. When I got home, I checked my files, found the details of the VW's purchase, and forwarded them to Mother. Dad had bought the car in Germany, but we repaid him in full when we took ownership in Savannah. Case closed.

By 1980, my file folders were so thick, it sometimes took me an hour or more to find the item I needed, so I started keeping a supplementary file on index cards like my former professor. I built a wooden box about six inches long thinking I'd never fill that up. Soon the small box gave way to three, eighteen-inch-long boxes. They were chock-full in two years. One day I said something to the departmental secretary about the "critical mess" my cards had reached, and she suggested checking the campus warehouse where surplus furniture was stored until it could be auctioned. This was about the time that the library and school administration were beginning to phase out those perforated IBM cards, which users were instructed not to "fold, spindle, or mutilate." In the warehouse, I found a four-foot-tall steel cabinet for three-by-seven-and-a-quarter-inch cards, convinced the manager I needed it for "research," and wrestled it into the trunk. Today I have five steel cabinets, the combined contents of which come as close as any insentient thing ever has to dominating my life. My cars, bicycles, house, and power tools don't even come close. I've joked with friends about an intervention, but if they followed through, I would be as forlorn as one of the recipients of a prefrontal lobotomy. The file is frankly an extension of my brain. My wife is a third lobe, but that's another story.

A born collector, this taxophile has gone through life with a plankton net, as Annie Dillard once suggested. If the house caught fire and I were home alone, I wouldn't save the picture albums, passports, or bank files; I'd save my card file. Without it, my memory falls somewhere between that of a goldfish (three seconds) and a squirrel (two weeks). In fact, the image of me digging in a file like a squirrel hunting an acorn buried six months earlier is another thing that prompted me to start collecting in a more systematic way.

Though retired from full-time teaching for five years now, I still spend an hour or two a day maintaining the file. As I read, I mark passages for saving. When my wife is finished with the same piece (I'm describing the ideal here), I usually cut out the statistic, quotation, poem, picture, or cartoon, and then drop it in a box by my desk. When I have twenty or thirty items, I glue them to a card, label it, and file it safely away. If the item is too large for a card, it goes in a file folder. Early on in the process with the inspiration of a topical quotation dictionary to thank, I appropriated the system of ordering things by broad idea—automobiles, energy, fundamentalism, democracy, homosexuality, comedy—and so forth. My index now has 2,200 categories (from Abbreviations, Abortion, and Absolutes to Zodiac, Zoning, and Zoos) while the file itself contains somewhere above 70,000 cards on which I've glued or written about 400,000 items.

When I prepare to write anything from my next essay to a condolence letter, I pull out the cards pertinent to my themes, stir the pot, and see what bubbles to the surface. The result is usually something very different from what I originally conceived. As Linus Pauling, winner of Nobel Prizes for Chemistry and Peace, once observed, "The best way to have a good idea is to have lots of ideas." The cards insure that I review the accepted wisdom before bombinating in a quantum void.

Perhaps a hypothetical example will help to explain the value of what is often called a "commonplace book" except that in my case "the book" is kept on file cards for ease of shuffling and free association. For a couple of years, nothing has tickled our three grandsons more than a fart joke, so should I write a story or essay for their amusement, I would open the "F" drawer, pull out the "Fart" cards (there are forty-eight of them), read through about 250 items, and start writing. Among the items I've saved are: an ad for Walter the Farting Dog (2007) by William Kotzwinkle; a reminder that in team cycling, one rider "breaks wind" for the others; the story of Babe Ruth being asked by a society matron if he'd care for some asparagus. Said Ruth, "No, thanks, it makes my farts smell funny"; a reminder that mooning the soccer referee is a "fragrant foul"; another ad, this one for the Flatulence Cushion with an activated-charcoal filter; a note that our son wrote his mother on her birthday saying, "I hope you like this card…Someone farted in the Hallmark shop, and I could only hold my breath long enough to grab this one"; a newspaper clipping about a South African flight with three hundred passengers sharing a compartment with seventy-two pigs, which had to turn back when the animals' exhaust set off the smoke alarm; the clever definition of "flatulence" as "the emergency vehicle that picks you up after being struck by a steamroller"; and finally my own observation that farting with impunity is the only good thing about mowing the lawn. With a repository such as this, my writing should be as relaxed as passing wind in the shower, and it usually is.

Incidentally, as I was reviewing the fart cards, I found "Poot" scrawled on one card in the handwriting of Spencer, our youngest grandson. I'd been outed by a ten-year-old.

If neither of our children wants the file after I'm gone, I've informed the special collections librarian that the school may have it. It's a consolation to me that other writers may one day use it to break out of a slump. Like the mulched leaves I dig into my vegetable garden, I hope to be fertile in decay. Somewhere on the exterior of the first file cabinet, I'd like the following words to be placed, "It's okay. It was all so beautiful. Whenever you read this, I will be there." I found that anonymous quotation in the "Grief" cards.

THE PARALLEL UNIVERSE: FICTION AND LIFE

"Reality is that which, when you stop believing in it, doesn't go away."
—Philip K. Dick

"Human kind cannot bear very much reality."
—T. S. Eliot

One fine Saturday morning in the autumn of my years, our son suggested a bike ride through the old neighborhoods where we'd once lived. Apparently, Shane, who was visiting from Columbia, had planned the ride because he'd brought his bike with him. About five miles from home, we made a half-mile loop around the Lake Hartwell YMCA where he and his sister played soccer and baseball thirty years ago.

"You want to go around *again*?" I asked.

"Yeah, I have lots of good memories out here." So we rode around two more times.

Later, as we neared the area behind the Clemson House, Shane asked, "Wanna spin by the old homestead?"

"Sure, but you know the houses are all gone—the university tore them down last year because it was going to cost more to re-fit them." Climbing the Daniel Drive hill, we saw perhaps ten people sitting at a portable table right where we'd lived for twelve years. There's nothing unusual about people tailgating anywhere around this football-silly town in the fall, but for some reason, these ten were sitting quietly alone eating breakfast in what was once a fifty-acre neighborhood for a hundred or more families with the kickoff five hours away. I said something with more irony than wit about "the nerve of those intruders," but Shane didn't hear me. He's lost a good bit of his hearing owing to Meniere's disease, and in the wind, he's almost deaf.

At the bottom of the Daniel hill, Shane said, "This is where I used to wait for you." Back in the early seventies, years before most of us had a cell phone, Shane would sit on his bike for thirty minutes or more waiting for my return home. I was taking graduate courses at the University of South Carolina, but I had promised the family I would make it home every Friday before dinner. My heart raced every time I spotted Shane on his bike at the corner of Daniel Drive and SC 93. As soon as he saw me, he'd sprint off and try to beat me home. I slowed to be sure he did.

"And I looked forward to seeing you here," I replied, "waiting on that old purple bike of yours with the banana seat and the ape-hanger handlebars." We rode on, but the traffic starting to build for the game cut our conversation short.

A week later, I was re-reading *The Catcher in the Rye* when I came to the part where Holden is telling his psychoanalyst about his younger brother Allie. Before the boy died, Holden said that he was playing golf one summer at a country club, and he had this premonition if he turned around he'd see Allie. Sure enough, there was his brother sitting on his bicycle outside the club fence just watching his sibling. "God," Holden tells his doctor, "he was a nice kid…"

Tears started rolling down my cheeks as I lay in bed reading beside my sleeping wife. I pulled the sleeve of my t-shirt up and blotted my eyes. Holden had the same problem; he was always choking up thinking of Allie or his younger sister riding the carrousel in Central Park.

Shortly after I'd finished Salinger's novel when I was in high school, I was caught speeding and paid a fifty-dollar fine. It didn't matter that the main reason I was hustling home was to make my father's 8 o'clock curfew. Nor did it matter that the radar caught me going seven miles per hour over the limit in a rural speed trap. Dad, who was not quite as distant as Holden's father, grounded me for the summer. Then to keep me "occupied," he had me blowtorch our plywood split-level, scrape off the old paint, prime it, and repaint. It took me three months because working under the eaves with a three-inch brush was to quote Holden, a "goddam" imposition. The summer before I went off to college, Salinger had taught me to swear, and I had ample time to practice over the roar of my blowtorch. I amused myself on the ladder of my penance by rehearsing words like "clavichord" (that still kills me), "grool" ("girl" + "ghoul"?), and the various inflections of "goddam."

I promised myself I was going to be a different father; indeed, I was going to make sure the park ducks had a place to go in the winter. When Shane said that he and his friend Mike wanted to ride their bikes to California and fly home after their high school graduation, I convinced them to take advantage of the prevailing westerlies: "Fly first," I advised, "and then ride with the wind at your back." Frankly, I was afraid he'd fall in love with the West Coast or some girl in one of those "butt-twitcher" dresses that Holden fell for.

My argument prevailed, and before the boys left on their cross-country adventure, I typed up "The Song of the Open Road" and several other poems to relieve the tedium of Texas. I had just taught *Catcher* in the spring, and I loved what Allie had done: copy his favorite poems on his baseball glove in green ink so that when there was a lull in the game, he'd have something to read in the outfield. To commemorate that, I bought Shane a green baseball glove, but I don't think he ever wrote any more than his name on it.

I didn't say anything at the start of this, but Shane came home alone this time because his wife has taken a dislike to my wife and me. "I still love you," she wrote us, "I just don't like you anymore." It's a long story, and Shane's caught in the middle, bless his heart, right where I was when my wife and mother used to quarrel. Fixing that rift between us and our daughter-in-law is about as likely as the task Holden had set for himself—erasing all the "fuck you" signs that his angry peers scrawled on the collapsing walls of their world. I used to rub off an average of one a month in the elevators where I worked, but when the words are scratched in stainless steel, it's goddam hopeless.

Hype Springs Eternal: Exaggeration

"Do not exaggerate...in military dispatches (before the battle)...."
—Lance Morrow

"Exaggeration may be helpful...in military dispatches (after the battle)...."
—Lance Morrow

In 1955, one blazing summer day, my friend Harold rode out from High Point, NC with two of his pals to watch the planes take off and land at a small rural airport. Returning home on their cast-iron Schwinns, the three seventh-graders, who had left home without their canteens, ran out of "gas." They stopped, therefore, at a farm house to beg for water, but no one was home. Harold then wandered into the garden where he spied a cucumber that was going to seed. After a long swig from the hose, he pulled the engorged vegetable free from its vine, cut it in two, and hollowed out a snug recess in the cut end. He then placed the green exclamation over his thumb and stuck his hand out in traffic. Before long, a farmer in a pickup stopped, let the boys throw their bikes in the back, and drove them still laughing back to town.

My friend's "green thumb" was a silent signpost put to excellent use, for without it, *they might have died out there!* (I exaggerate, of course.) I like to think that the driver of the truck saw the oversized "thumb," chuckled to himself, and thought, "These clever boys are worth saving." I imagine it was a little like driving across the Great Plains, looking up, and seeing those sixty-foot faces on Mt. Rushmore, the nation's four sculptured expletives.

Southern dialect does not lack for hyperbole, which often makes for comically effective discourse, for we frequently think that if speakers can make us laugh, they must have a point. Take my maternal grandmother: "Go fetch me some potatoes from the basement, Skippa," she used to say, "can't you see I'm busy as a moth in a mitten." "Dear," as we called her, was "country as corn flakes," and I loved her for it. My Georgia grandfather "Papa" liked to conclude a tall tale with, "If that ain't a fact, God is a possum!" I reckon he used up his quota of exclamations sometime in his twenties, which may be an exaggeration, but then I wasn't there for the tally.

When I was teaching composition, I sometimes used the following description of Table Rock Mountain drawn from the *Camden [SC] Gazette* (June 6, 1819) because many of my students had climbed the nine-hundred-foot knob visible from the roof of our building. "Very few persons," the anonymous journalist wrote, "who have once cast a glimpse into the almost boundless abyss can again exercise sufficient fortitude to approach the margin of the chasm. Almost everyone on looking over involuntarily falls to the ground senseless, nerveless and helpless..." One can only guess what the writer would have said about the immensity Tibetans call Chomolungma (29,035'). Indeed, over the years, I've never met anyone who was struck unconscious by the view from *any* "mountain" in South Carolina perhaps because the tallest rises only 3,533 feet. A few years ago, Sassafras stood about thirty feet taller, but the state graded the top to make it more accessible.

"Over-egging the pudding" often has an effect contrary to what a cook hopes to evoke. The same might be said of writers who plump their puddings with hyperbole. Whether it's real estate ("Adorable rental property"), advertising ("JOY [perfume] adds length to my legs, wit to my conversation, and a better accent to my French"), or sportscasting ("He could catch a peppercorn in the dark!"), the grander the arc of the embellishment, the sooner I tune it out because the sooner the lie is evident.

Several years ago, I led a group of alumni to Venice where one woman was prepared to purchase a dozen Murano glasses. However, when the perspiring salesman exclaimed, "Water will taste like wine from these goblets, madam," his customer snorted and left the premises. Indeed, hype has it consequences as every salesman can attest. As a poet whose ear is more sympathetic to Robert Frost, I admire Gerard Manley Hopkins, but I do not love him. A typical Frostian line, effective as it is understated, might be, "The woods are lovely, dark, and deep,/ but I have promises to keep." Hopkins, on the other hand, prefers an overstressed line like, "Brute beauty and valour and act, oh, air, pride, plume, here/ buckle!" I find this breathless verse falling on my ear like the strokes of midnight on an insomniac.

Of course, my ear is of little consequence in the grand scheme of things, but anyone who has ever read a stack of résumés knows how quickly the discard pile grows reading all those unsupported claims of greatness. Words like "outstanding," "exceptional," "excellent," "driven," and "energetic," it's safe to say, doom an application from the start. It's far better for the evaluators to come to their own conclusions based on the concrete evidence supplied, not the adjectives.

Perhaps the strongest case against hype was made in 2002 when former CIA director George Tenet assured President George W. Bush that Saddam Hussein had weapons of mass destruction. How sure of the intelligence was he, one staffer asked. It's a "slam dunk," the director replied, drawing a metaphor from basketball when a shot is driven home with such force that the glass backboard may shatter on the floor. Three years after no WMDs had been found and several thousand Americans and Iraqis had been killed in the war, Tenet admitted, "Those were the two dumbest words I ever said."

Understatement, the rhetorical opposite of hyperbole, is far more effective in closing an argument. When ad writers for Rolls-Royce wanted to make the case that their luxury sedan had a powerful motor, they wrote, "The horsepower of the Rolls-Royce is adequate." And when Emperor Showa (Hirohito) reported to the Japanese people that Hiroshima, Nagasaki, and most of their inhabitants had vanished from the Earth, he said, "The war situation has developed not necessarily to Japan's advantage." A few weeks later, he admitted that he'd been posing as the son of a god for years.

Just as the portions laid out on Leonardo's table in *The Last Supper* have grown larger with every "restoration," so have religious savants occasionally over-egged wisdom literature. To cite one instance, Luke quotes Jesus saying that Christians should "hate" their families and follow him. ("If any man come to me, and hate not his father, and mother, and wife, and children, and brethren, and sisters, yea, and his own life also, he cannot be my disciple." KJV) I once suggested to a Presbyterian minister that "hate" might have been an ill-chosen word. The good pastor said, "Oh, that's just hype." But if hyperbole is an overstatement in the service of truth, it is nigh impossible to know the truth of Luke 14:26. Personally, I think Jesus might have learned something from the Japanese emperor who acknowledged that he felt much "lighter" once he'd given responsibility for the world back to Mother Nature.

From Pegasus to Pegasaurus: Myth

"Myth is nothing more than ancient gossip."
—Stanislaw Lec

"The goal of the myth is to [affect] a reconciliation of the individual consciousness with the universal will."
—Joseph Campbell

If "an anecdote is the first draft of myth, a lump of cold steel awaiting its smith," here's a story for you to hammer on. Maybe there was and maybe there wasn't a beauty named Calypso, an embittered mother who named her daughter after the toxic orchid or the nymph of the sacred spring; opinions differ. What is known is the girl's father was a handsome but brawling sailor from the Greek isles, her mother, a flower peddler from Kingston. However, after drowning Calypso and molesting Arethusa, the nameless sailor abandoned his child and returned to the sea. With skin the color of caramel and jet-black eyes, the orphaned girl was raised a Rastafarian with dreadlocks into which she wove skins of Jamaican boas. With her waist-length hair, she seduced and strangled the men who closely resembled herself. Perhaps she succeeded in finding her father, perhaps not.

One of the beauties of myth is the way past and present are united. Anyone who recalls the pre-Christian punishment of Sisyphus, for example, will "catch" the allusion whether the modern sufferer is an unhappy vacationer pushing a beach ball up a sand dune or an office worker deleting "tons of spam" only to see it return. Myth, then, is a bridge we cross to discover that what it meant to be human in Homer's day is the same for Homer Simpson.

Of course, if one has never been exposed to literature beyond the Bible, one cannot be expected to understand the foreign mythic reference. When a Christian neighbor complained that the rain kept washing the rocks down the slopes of her rock garden forcing her to carry them back up, she could only frown when I called her "Miss Sisyphus" and accused her of loving her labors.

I was fortunate in that Edith Hamilton's *Mythology* was one of the first serious books I read for a freshman Latin class, so the classical allusions in Milton and Keats came easily to me when I discovered them in literature classes. Many years later after reading Joseph Campbell's *The Power of Myth*, I dipped into Chinese mythology, but it was too late. Nothing would stick, no one understood my allusions to the Jade Emperor, and I quickly lost interest. A new mythology is really a new language or means of communicating, and the window for acquiring it is very small.

Campbell, the godfather of modern myth studies, often recommended living mythically. To wring the most from life, he suggested that we think of our oatmeal as ambrosia, our coffee and orange juice as nectar, our subway commute as a trip through Hades, tossing a Frisbee in the park as play in the Elysian Fields, our annual tax routine as Sisyphean, and the neighbor's dog as Cerberus. As I have written elsewhere, "Hell is not so dark when 'Cerberus' barks," especially if you know it's the beagle puppy next door. When our son was small and wondered why the wind blew, introducing Aeolus, the Greek god with a bag full of wind, was a lot easier for me and more satisfying for him than explaining pressure differentials. His mother Aphrodite, a distant Aeolian cousin, agreed, and it provided me more time to follow the Herculean but ultimately saturnine efforts of the Ursa Minors.

As that last sentence implies, English is saturated with Greek, Roman, and Scandinavian myth. We took our names for the days from Norse myth and our months from the Romans. And while few study Greek anymore, the river Lethe is still flowing lethargically, Pan is still piping away in a "panic," Aphrodite is present in every "aphrodisiac," Hermes and Aphrodite are linked to every unfortunate "hermaphrodite," and Thespis is still acting out in "thespian." Up at the top of every human spine sits the cupped "hands" of the Atlas vertebra holding our skulls the way the Titan prisoner was condemned to support the heavens.

In a crotchet called "Seattle Homespun," I come at myth from another angle: "Wool yarn woven from a greasy skein/ shields its wearers from the freezing rain." Dry and warm is about all one can ask from a sweater, but a fine "woolen" myth provides spiritual comfort as well. During WWII, my wife was growing up with her brother in a German village near the industrial city of Braunschweig. When the larger town was bombed near Christmas of 1944, the village folk could see the flames twenty miles away. The children were naturally terrified, but their mother—like all the village mothers—assured them that the flames on the horizon were simply thousands of Christmas trees with all their wax candles burning at once.

Some would call that story a lie, but I prefer to think of it as a myth or fable that allowed two children a few hours of dreamless sleep in their bomb shelter. Christopher Hitchens, who made a living from being a professional wet blanket, may have been able to tell his grandchildren that their dead grandmother is food for worms, but I'll tell mine, if the day comes, that there's another star glittering in a darkling sky. The fear of death is why myth and religion have always stolen a march on science, and I don't see that tactical advantage changing even as technology progresses.

Myth and science have been at odds for millennia because if you think about it, there's not much difference between the Olympians pulling a few strings for Aeneas and half the globe suspended upside down with no strings attached. Millions of Americans have invested heavily in Jesus's return, "one nation indivisible," and time travel, but the likelihood of any in this trio being realized is slim.

Every religion is a custodian of a myth set or "necessary fiction" as Wallace Stevens called it. The historical-scientific truth of the set is of no consequence; in most cases there's a little fact mixed with a lot of fiction—just enough of the former to make the latter credible. But whether the oral tale was first spoken by Homer, Jesus, or my mother-in-law, the upshot is that if the story is retold or written down, it's because it provides the satisfying illusion of control.

I began this essay by casting a mythic tale involving a woman's search for her rogue father. This quest is so universal and primal that it's called an archetype, or the original mold from which countless copies have been and continue to be cast. When Telemachus, Oedipus, Pearl (in *The Scarlet Letter*), Pinocchio, Jesus, and Luke Skywalker went looking for their fathers the way Arethusa searched for hers, Carl Jung thought they were all following unconscious patterns the brain had inherited over eons of bad fathers pursued by diligent children wanting some answers or revenge.

One reason I write these essays is in response to what I call the breadcrumb theory of fatherhood. One day, I expect, some Hansel or Gretel will come looking for me just as I have plumbed the historical record for some clue to the first Eisenmengers in the New World. Each essay is a crumb I scatter, so one day my descendants can find some answers. I can't think of a better reason to transcribe the myth of myself. Just wish I had the questions in advance.

The Hyena's Share: Diner Slang

"Slang is the growth bud of language."
—The Wordspinner

"Anyone who doesn't know a foreign language knows nothing of his own."
—Goethe

If you've been following Slim's hard times in *Gasoline Alley,* you surely recall his initiation at Corky's Diner. The grill man's first order that morning was for "Adam and Eve on a raft; baled hay and a cup of naked!" This was followed by "a light crust doughboy and SOS! Hurry!" Said Slim in his befuddlement, "*Hurry* is the only part of these orders I understand!" Knowing that her tips depended on the speed of Slim's output, the server explained in the following strip that the first order was for poached eggs on toast, shredded wheat, and black coffee; the second called for light toast and "shit on a shingle." Of course, no newspaper that buries *Doonesbury* in the classified ads as the *Greenville News* does is going to run a strip with a profane remnant of Old English, so the artist Jim Scancarelli was forced to gloss SOS. as "chipped beef on toast." I'm sure some readers are still wondering why it wasn't "CBT" along the well known lines of "BLT" or "PBJ." The bigger mystery is how "SOS." slipped by the censors.

The point is that Americans are endlessly inventive when it comes to nicknaming food and drink whether in a diner, the school cafeteria, or the household kitchen. I've never made a formal study of it, but I'm quite sure that food slang occupies at least a hyena's share of any slang dictionary like Cassel's or Partridge. Only the lions—namely sex, alcohol, and excretion—devour more room.

In the 1959, I heard my first example of diner slang when placing an order for a hamburger with lettuce, tomato, and onion at Atlanta's Varsity Drive-In. Before I could order my drink, the clerk at the register turned to the phalanx of short-order-cooks behind her, and yelled, "Run a burger through the garden." I was in love as surely as Hemingway loved the bullfights and I've been an aficionado ever since. As a teen, if I was feeling frisky, my friends and I would pull into a drive-in and order a "pine float" and drive off before the glass of water and toothpick arrived. I was naïve enough to think the order would be filled. If I were especially brave, I'd order a "virgin Coke" instead of a "cherry."

Years later realizing how much I owed to diner culture, I wrote the following doggerel called "The Comfort-Food Diner":

The cook's name is Mac,
the waitress says, "Hon',"
and next to the napkins
lie a few crumbs—
I'm back in Mac's Diner
feeling like someone.

One of my students caught the diner-slang bug, and after a summer
of working the counter at the old Pavilion in Myrtle Beach, he came by
with several new items like "Gimme a dog, hold the fleas," which is a hot
dog without onions, and "burn a cow, make her cry," which is a well-done
burger with extra onions. Asked my student, "Why do I feel like the last
speaker of Yiddish?"

Alas, most of the places like the Pavilion and Mac's have yielded to the
big chains where a small order of fries is "to go," not mounted "on wheels,"
fitted for "boots," or equipped to "fly." What seems to be enjoying a revival,
however, is food slang dressed up or down. Fish has been "brain food" for
decades, but now noodle soup and cauliflower are "brain food" as well.
Cheerios are "donut seeds"; pickles are reborn as "cucumbers that refuse to
die," raisins have morphed into "grapes with a sunburn," and celery is "the
next best thing to eating nothing." Sushi that once had an Eastern cachet is
now "bait," but according to *Time,* proletarian pasta is now "the apotheosis
of flour and water." Coffee, which in diner slang was "java" or "joe," has
climbed the social ladder to "black nectar of the white gods." That will
come as a surprise to the brown-skinned natives of Mocha and Bogota.
The shift is even affecting Southern dialect: the old "seven-course meal"
(a six-pack and a possum) is now a half-dozen Krispy Kremes and coffee.

If diner slang in the 1930s and 40s was designed for efficiency of communication, the newer food slang is mostly for show. In the 1980s, Chan-
dler's By Night, a specialty sandwich restaurant in Greenville, staked its
existence on pop culture, but the menu was tastier than the food, and it has
since folded. A student managed to smuggle out a menu where I learned
that "The Rev. Moon" featured "a lot of bologna on pumpernickel." "The
Sophia Loren" offered "a tempting breast of turkey on brown bread." And
"The Strom Thurmond," a hometown favorite, was piled with "aged beef
and American cheese." Another restaurant, whose name I have lost, offered the "Ollie" sandwich in the summer of 1987 when all tongues were
wagging about Col. Oliver North. The "Ollie" consisted of "red-blooded
American beef on a hero bun with shredded lettuce topped with an American flag." If the cloyed "Ollie" had still been around in 2003, it might well
have been served with a side of Freedom Fries.

If "patriotism," as Lin Yutang observed, is another word for the food we grew up on, it should come as no surprise to find some cross-border sniping. The ancient rivalry between the Old World and the New is reflected in "burn the British," the diner call for a toasted English muffin. Similar animosities, I expect, are found around the world.

Most food slang is diplomatically neutral. If a German orders "solid beer with liquid bread," he's just having a slice of sour-dough rye with his Löwenbrau, not maligning French beer or Polish bread. Italians may not like the fact that some Americans in the Northeast used to call a hero sandwich a "Garibaldi," but it was just another innocuous item on the menu. Only a neo-con would object to a sandwich in Rome called the "George Washington."

Permit me to close with a story that subtly captures the affection most of us feel toward many of the terms I've discussed. When an uncle of my friend Malcolm Usrey moved from Alabama to Texas in the 1930s, he piled his farm implements and sons into a boxcar while his wife and mother rode coach. Every fifty miles or so, the train would pull into a station to allow passengers to grab a bite to eat since there was no dining car. After an unusually brief stop, the engineer blew the whistle, and the conductor shouted, "All aboard!"

"Oh dear," the wife exclaimed, "my coffee's too hot to drink, and the train's leaving."

A gallant old farmer in overalls stood up and said, "Here you go ma'm, drink mine. It's done been saucered and blowed."

Word Clay: Wordplay

Surely most Sunday school graduates know that Genesis begins in wordplay: Adam introduces himself to the creature bloodlessly excised from his flank saying, "Madam, I'm Adam," and his quivering mate shyly replies, "Eve." (I should say that I'm using a very rare edition of the Bible that's long out of print.) From this brief introduction, the complexity multiplies. The serpent, the embodiment of *evil,* is *live.* Get it? Some call such an odd pair a *semordnilap.* Get it? When Jehovah sends the first two humans out of Eden, He utters the shortest sentence possible in English, "Go!" He might have palindromicly added, "Am I as stupid and impetuous as you are?" but Jehovah is not a deity to renege on his word, so the sentence went uncommuted.

Once the precedent was established, Eve's descendants started collecting miscellanea as if they were shards of the Holy Grail. Here is a dollop of my own collection:

- *dollop*: A delicious invertogram

- *kinnikinnik*: A ground cover in the American Northwest also known as "bear-berry." It's the longest single-word palindrome in *Webster's Third International.*

- *NOON*: A mirror palindrome

- *MAT*: A word that is vertically symmetrical

- *DOCK*: A word that is horizontally symmetrical

- *OX*: A word in which the letters are horizontally and vertically symmetrical

- *dust*: One of about thirty English contranyms, a word that means one thing and its opposite as in, "Dust the mantle, Jeeves, and then dust the tomato vines."

• *baloney, balony, bologna, bologny, boloney:* The only word with one pronunciation that has five alternate spellings.

• *dord:* An example of a ghost word (in this case meaning "density") invented by lexicographers to see if anyone is stealing their database.

• *Elvis:* An anagram for *lives*, need I say more? For those still on his trail, he's probably wearing Levis.

• *I:* The most common word in English, and a reflection of our gargantuan ego. The Germans never have understood why we capitalize it.

• *TWENTY-NINE*: An eerie word made with twenty-nine straight strokes of the pen. The Germans quibble with that hyphen.

• *queueing:* The longest common word with five vowels in a row— you'd go broke buying vowels for this word. I cannot blame those who prefer *queuing*.

• *archaeoaeolotropic:* The longest word in English with six vowels in a row. It means "a piece of ancient material that is not equally elastic when pulled in different directions."

• *abstemiously*: One of a handful of words with all six vowels in alphabetical order

• *squirrelled*: The longest one-syllable word in English, meaning "saved" or "hamstered"

• *-ough*: With nine ways to pronounce it, this is the most flexible syllable in the language. Try saying aloud, "A rough, dough-faced, but thoughtful ploughman, strode the streets of Scarborough. After falling in a slough, he coughed and hiccoughed."

• *billowy*: The longest common word whose letters are all in alphabetical order

• *cuspidor*: The most beautiful word in the language according to

James Joyce, a writer to whom context meant little. Wilfred Funk nominated *asphodel*, but I prefer the punchier *spork*.

• *smegma*: The most disgusting word in the language, meaning a secretion of the mammalian genitals. Apparently, the Los Angeles experimental noise group with the same name agrees.

• *thousand*: The first number word to use an *a*

• *therein*: The seven-letter word with the most English words contained therein without altering the order of the letters. See if you can find all ten.

• *deeded*: The longest third-order isogram, a word in this case with three *e*'s and three *d*'s

• *frillless*: The shortest word with three identical consonants in a row; as often as I have written this word, I still think it needs a hyphen.

• *language*: The answer to the old riddle: "Think of three words ending in *–gry*. *Angry* and *hungry* are two of them. There are only three words in the English language. What is the third? The word is something everyone uses every day."

• *pumpernickel*: The best etymology ever; in German it's the bread that makes one "pass wind like the devil."

• *set*: The English word that has the most definitions. The *Oxford English Dictionary* has twenty-six pages worth!

• *floccinaucinihilipilification*: The longest word in the *Oxford English Dictionary* meaning "the action or habit of estimating as worthless"

• *pneumonoultramicroscopicsilicovolcanoconiosis*: A synonym for silicosis as if it needed one. It's also the longest word in *Webster's Third International* meaning a lung disease caused by volcanic dust. There's also a 1,913 letter-long chemical name, but that has not made it into any dictionary, and that is as it should be.

• *Nymphs vex, beg quick fjord waltz*: The shortest pangraph or sentence with twenty-seven letters using all twenty-six letters, but who spells the Swedish *Ford* with a *j*? Fame and wealth await the word spinner who can eliminate that extra *e*.

• *07734*: An upside-down and backward number word assuming the *4* has no diagonal, but my font selection is limited—"Damn it to 7734!"

• *squinched* and *strengths*: The two longest words pronounced as single syllables

• *rhythms*: The longest word without an *a, e, i, o,* or *u*

• *she*: Named by the American Dialect Society the "word of the millennium," 1000-2000, because Old English did not have a third-person personal pronoun exclusively for women before about 1200 AD

• *jazz*: Named by the A.D.S. the best new word of 1900–2000

• *web*: Named by the A.D.S. the best new word of 1990–2000

• *mix*: The largest Roman numeral word, which is worth 1009

• *Wood John Mass*: A rebus, or a representation of a word, phrase, or in this case an address by pictures, symbols, or in this case the placement of the words. Supposedly, a letter addressed as shown was delivered to John Underwood of Andover, Massachusetts. Since there is no street listed, I assume the postman knew this fellow or Andover was very small.

• *zyzzyva*: The last word in any major dictionary; it's an American weevil.

• suprapreantepenultimate: Word meaning "fifth to the last" and the only word composed of five prefixes

• reliable: Rare English word in current formal usage that as recently as the nineteenth century was considered unacceptable because of its Scottish origins. No one thinks "reliable" is unacceptable today.

• spot: Eisiminger's blend-coinage meaning "spicy hot" to fill the gaping and inexcusable lacuna. Consider this my gift to the language which has given so much without charge.

• uncopyrightable: Longest word in English that can be spelled without repeating a letter

• Leodensian: The least expected demonym in English; a resident of Leeds, England

• irregardless: Rightfully shunned by the literate but no more redundant than unravel and debone, which are commonplace

• hydroxydesoxycorticosterone and hydroxydeoxycorticosterones: Longest anagrams in English

• homesickness: Longest single-word calque or loan-word translation in English; from the German Heimweh

• the n-word: In its dysphemistic form, this is the verbal equivalent of cyanide; no English word is more toxic. Even this euphemistic form should be used with great caution.

• its and it's: The most commonly misspelled and confused words in English

• inflammable: The most dangerous word in English which is also inoffensive; many think the word means "not flammable" when it means "highly flammable."

Leonardo da Vinci, Roberto Guatelli speculated, simultaneously drew with his right hand even as he was writing backwards with the left. It's the only way this contemporary scholar could imagine the famed painter-sculptor-engineer accomplishing all that he did. In other words, Dan Brown got it all wrong! Leonardo was not a descendant of Mary Magdalene, wife of Jesus; he was a child of Eve, the matron saint of all who see words as keys to locks. But these are no ordinary locks, as I have tried to show above. These have tumblers worthy of the savants among us.

As Was Said of Old: Proverbs

"There's an old proverb that says just about anything you want it to."
—Anonymous

"Solomon made a book of proverbs, but a book of proverbs never made a Solomon."
—English proverb

I suppose the empty nest had something to do with it, but after our daughter graduated from the University of South Carolina and moved to New York, I started feeling guilty about all the great advice I'd never given her. So I went to my files and distilled a list of what I claimed were "Pop's Proverbs." The Chinese say, "The palest ink trumps the best memory," so I placed it first to encourage writing. Among other things, I advised her to plow around the stumps of Manhattan, to forgive herself over and over, and not to wait for people to love her. I reminded her that civility costs nothing, that there's an exception to most rules, that the end usually does not justify the means, and that pretty is as pretty does.

She wrote back in the palest ink saying thank you, but she'd assimilated most everything I'd collected long before she left home. Apparently "Pop" had conveyed the wisdom through his actions, making the precepts redundant. As Anja put it, "Pop had planted seeds rather than scattering pearls under foot."

Still, a well-turned maxim has an enduring charm. Something must be working because many English proverbs have their roots in cultures long dead, yet these survivors show no signs of root rot. Wolfgang Mieder, the dean of American paremiology, has said that the average American is familiar with about three hundred proverbs. And what exactly are they? Think of the experience of a million people compacted over a thousand years into a linguistic diamond. This figure may help to explain the rarity and staying power of the form. It may also explain why Ben Franklin, one of America's finest aphorists, preferred, "A drop of reason to a flood of words." Of course, D. H. Lawrence thought Franklin a "snuff-colored" simpleton for trying to reduce complex moral opinions to a sentence, but then Lawrence never edited an almanac either.

I expect the Bible is what most Americans think of when proverbs are mentioned. Solomon wrote some three thousand, and even though the disciples urged Jesus to speak "plainly," his parables are scattered with metaphorical gems like "a house divided cannot stand."

Occasionally editors simplify a proverb, and their pruning changes its meaning. *The Penguin Dictionary of Epigrams* includes, "Men do not despise a thief, if he steal to satisfy his soul when he is hungry." (Proverbs 6:30) When I read this, I assumed Solomon was defending one who robs the rich and gives to the poor. But if one reads the next verse, omitted in the Penguin edition, the sense is strongly qualified: "Yet if [the thief] is caught, he must pay back seven times more—he must give up everything he has." Suddenly the only thing wrong with robbing the rich is getting caught, and Solomon resembles the Sheriff of Nottingham.

As an occasional Bible reader, I've long admired Ezekiel for confronting Moses's misguided proverb in Deuteronomy, "The sins of the fathers shall be visited on the sons even to the…fourth generation." Nonsense, says Ezekiel, the wickedness of the wicked shall befall the wicked, not his innocent offspring. I've often wondered what this later prophet with his emphasis on personal responsibility would have thought of God's only son dying for another's sins. Unfortunately, we'll never know.

In the Bible and elsewhere, the realities of the moralist are often subtly expressed. Many writers of wisdom literature urge us to trust the deity, but most know how some shorn lambs have shivered to death in places like Auschwitz. As a result, Americans are advised to "trust God but keep your gunpowder dry." The Arabs append, "…but tie your camels tight." Gamblers warn, "…but cut the cards." Hindus caution, "…but row away from the rocks." Jews, still reeling from the Diaspora, urge, "Hope for a miracle but do not depend on one." And Russians delete miracles altogether bluntly stating, "Trust but verify."

It's interesting to me the way proverbs of one generation correct the oversights of another. For centuries, Germans told their nubile girls, "Children, church, and kitchen," for those were the provinces of women. Translated into English, the adage became, "A woman's place is in the home." Questions about church, should they arise, would be answered by a husband when he came home from work. In the American South, the proverb deteriorated into, "Keep 'em barefoot and pregnant" figuring poverty and pregnancy would keep women from temptation. After they were worn out by childbearing, there would be plenty of time for the church. In the late twentieth century, however, women rose up collectively and said, "Enough! A woman's place is in the House and Senate." This modern variation is even more effective on a t-shirt when "the Senate" is printed on the back. One day soon, "the Oval Office" may join it.

Other modern adaptations of the genre include the "incomplete proverb" finished by some suspiciously jaded eight-year-old, who writes, "A penny saved? Is not much." Then there's the "literal foreign proverb," such as, "One finger cannot open the anus." There's the "mean-spirited proverb,"

"Kick a blind man—why do any less than God has done." There's the "mal-appropriate proverb," "A bird in the hand is worth two in the ointment." There's the "virtual proverb," such as, "Too many clicks spoil the browse." There's the "paired proverb" such as, "All that glitters is not gold [English] because all is not butter that comes from a cow [Yiddish]." There's the "commercial proverb," "Different Volks for different folks." There's the "engorged proverb" used to illustrate the efficacy of brevity: compare, "Rectitude is its own remuneration," to, "Virtue is its own reward." There's the "comic proverb" such as Stephen Wright's, "If you had everything, where would you put it?" There's the "inverted proverb," "Time's fun when you're having flies." Finally, there's the "updated proverb": instead of "carrying coals to Newcastle," we in South Carolina "haul grits to Charleston."

To those who say that the era of the proverb has passed, I offer two examples in closing. The world would be a very different place today if George W. Bush had taken two Arab proverbs to heart before invading Iraq in 2003: "It takes one crazy man to block the well, but the whole village to remove the stones." And, "The local devils are better than angels from abroad."

Tales from the Cup and Chaucer: Punning Business Names

"In the pun, two strings of thought are tangled into one acoustic knot."
—Arthur Koestler

"Puns are the droppings of soaring wits."
—Victor Hugo

It all began quite innocently. One day Gudrun "Goody" Greef, found herself browsing for lingerie at Bare Assets; a few weeks later, she was studying the maternity clothes in Mother Frocker, and nine months later the clerk in Little Hang-Ups melted Gudrun's Visa card.

Gudrun's new husband, Solomon Gomorrah, was similarly afflicted. A short man, he bought his clothes at Napoleon's Closet. His barber was Julius Scissor; his favorite restaurant, Eats of Eden; his favorite bakery, Let Them Eat Cake; and his favorite pet shop, Barkingham Palace. Goody and Solomon, it seems, were compulsives of an odd tribe.

One day, however, while Solomon was in The Marquis de Suede, he sensed that the clerk, Uneeda Vest, would understand his problem, and his intuition proved accurate. In fact, Mr. Vest said he thought Solomon's compulsion not only common but harmless. He, for example, hired Partners in Grime to do his janitorial work, C'est Cheese to cater his annual Christmas party, and Traders of the Lost Art to decorate his store with antique dildos.

Another customer in the store, Miss Dee Meana, who'd overheard the conversation, said she had this curious disorder herself. "I never eat anywhere but A Deli Named Desire," she said. "And a couple times a year, I sneak in the back door of The Best Little Hair House in Town to get a perm."

About that time, Miss Meana's poodle tugged at her leash and barked. "Oh, yes," Dee said, "Pet Showfur drives Spike here through the park every afternoon, and I buy all her food at Little Arf 'n Annie."

That night Solomon told Gudrun of the conversation he'd had, and both breathed freely for the first time in weeks. They were not freaks or aberrations; in fact, they might even be normal. When Solomon read that George Washington had preferred to stay at Martha's Inn when he was away from Mt. Vernon, they felt positively vindicated. Thus began their concerted effort, for the closet door was open. The Yellow Pages turned to sheets of pure gold. Henceforth, the places where they shopped could be expensive or cheap, friendly or rude, but if they didn't have an adorably clever name, they didn't profit from the Gomorrah's business. When Solomon was transferred, he hired Mother Trucker to move them, and when

Gudrun's mirror was broken in the move, she called Kiss My Glass.

The veiled insults of former friends sailed over them without mussing their coifs. The Golden Pages were irresistible. Gudrun shopped blissfully for lingerie at The Pleasure Chest and Easter bonnets at Hats in the Belfry. Solomon happily hired Sherlock Tomes to find an out-of-print book, Maid to Order to help Gudrun with the housecleaning, and Eufloria to arrange the flowers at his mother's funeral. When their VCR began pleating the video tapes, he took the machine to Sherlock Ohms. Nevertheless, life was not a bowl of cherries from Currant Thymes. The Gomorrah's decline began with a large bill from Cut the Crepe after a party Gudrun threw for her bridge club. Then came bar bills for Solomon from Absinthe Makes the Heart Grow Fonder and credit-card bills for Gudrun from Dressed to Thrill. After a night at The Slipped Disco, there were medical bills. An ill-advised vacation at Paradise Casino led them to The Happy Hocker. The last financial straw, however, was a frivolous lawsuit that ruined Solomon's Here's Johnny portable-toilet business. These were desperate times, but it wasn't until Solomon caught himself buying a sombrero and a serape from El L. Bean and Gudrun signed up for aerobics at Bringing Up the Rear that they realized there was tarnish on the Golden Pages. Together they sought a support group.

They found one at Inn Cahoots where one weekend in the Poconos thirty people afflicted just like themselves bared their tormented souls. There was a New Ager who ran up huge bills at Sirius Fitness, a mystery-book lover who spent his entire paycheck at Murder Ink, and a tropical fish fan who changed his will to include Tanks-A-Lot. Poverty was the common denominator.

Gudrun and Solomon vowed that some financial, if not linguistic, changes would be made. Gudrun promised to shop at Déjà New. She canceled her contract with The Other Woman maid service, vowed to do her own laundry instead of sending it to Washbucklers, and started patronizing the Eat No Evil salad bar. Solomon agreed that henceforth he'd get his haircuts at The Clip Joint and eat at The Bare Bones.

But the strain proved too much for Solomon's heart. He collapsed and died after inhaling a cherry cheesecake at Just Desserts. Blinded by grief, Gudrun phoned The Baggit Funeral Parlor and The Sweet Chariot Helicopter Service to scatter his ashes. Today, she lives alone at Still Hopes Retirement Community. Once a month, she has her hair dyed blue at Curl Up and Dye.

(Note: all the business names above were drawn from the Yellow Pages.)

Yada, Yada, Yada, Cinderbella: Language Acquisition

"Language is a virus from outer space."
—William S. Burroughs

"The work of language deserves our greatest care, for the tongue's fire may devour the world or light the way."
—Scott Russell Sanders

I've read that children growing up on the streets of Johannesburg may absorb as many as ten languages or dialects by osmosis before they are twelve. Prior to the age of six, children are near-perfect language sponges: one swipe and most of the words on the countertop are gone. Our grandson Spencer in his first week of German-only kindergarten listened to his teacher read a book that introduced the class to ten German color words and animal names. That weekend, he and his mother chanced on the same book in English in a Charlotte library. Spencer recognized the book immediately, and as his Mother read the English, he translated every word into German, adding in English "the wolf is actually a dog only feistier."

In the thirteenth century, Frederick II decided to find out once and for all what language Adam and Eve spoke, so he ordered some of his subjects not to speak in the presence of their babies. Ultimately his majesty failed because, as the monk placed in charge of the experiment wrote, "He labored in vain, for the children could not live without clappings of the hands and gestures, and gladness of countenances, and blandishments," which included any speech, flattering or otherwise. Though the monk does not specify, some of the children may have become psychotic because that is what happened to apes in similar deprivation studies in the twentieth century.

Though linguists like Noam Chomsky will object, the infant's acquisition of language is magical, and it's not surprising that the Beat Generation novelist William S. Burroughs would attribute it to an extraterrestrial virus. We know that the process begins in the womb because neonates turn more often to their mothers' voices than any others. Moreover, French babies after being cut from their umbilicals cry with a rising contour while the cries of German babies fall. The best explanation is that the fetuses learn some of the rhythms of their native language eavesdropping in the third trimester. Once in the cradle, the rehearsal of vowels begins almost immediately—ah, ee, oh—three sounds fundamental to all languages on the globe. Consonants follow a few months later because there are twenty-two sites in the brain just for recognizing the difference between "bea" and "pea." Make those sounds with your own lips to see how subtly we articulate them without a millisecond of forethought.

The rehearsal of vowels is universal. In the first few months of life, the vocalizations of Chinese, Indian, and Italian babies are indistinguishable. But in short order, the babbling and the crying take on characteristics of the language or languages being spoken in the nursery. Fathers are often jealous that their offspring say "mama" before "dada," but the reason is simply that labials like "m" are learned before dentals like "d." All children learn to eat and speak in the front of their mouths before advancing to the back. Apparently, we are wired for that progression because all babies do it. Deaf children, bless their silent hearts, babble with their hands.

One result of this very intense concentration is that infants sleep fifteen hours or more each day. But the results of their work are soon noticeable: at eighteen months, they know about ten words; six months later they know fifty; and by six, they have a vocabulary of six thousand. It has been estimated that three-year-olds are acquiring a new word every ninety minutes they are awake. Just think, before some Neanderthals lucked on the FOXP2 gene in a random mutation, the most humans could probably say was, "We hunt." But this new language gene enabled our species to acquire the 250 words necessary to explain how to knapp a spear point or build a fire.

Every parent and grandparent labors under the illusion that their offspring are prodigies. As a student of the language for seven decades with two children and four grandchildren, I'm not above that misapprehension. Nevertheless, I have not tired of recording the milestones of our progeny. When Edgar, our oldest, was having difficulty pronouncing "Gramps," he improvised a binary code and began calling me "Not-Omi." ("Omi" is the name all our grandkids use for their German grandmother.) When Omi's mother died, Edgar's brother Sterling wrote, "I'm so sorry about your loss to your mom. I would be sad too if my mom died. I would miss her every day. Even though I never saw your mom in all my 10 years of living but if I did she would be the best great grandmother in the whole world." To keep the scales balanced, I won't say any more about Spencer except that he is in the fifth grade now and his German proficiency is exceeded only by his English.

Then there is Lena, our only granddaughter, whose head is perpetually shrouded in a flame-tinted cumulus, but inside the skies are blue. At eight months, her first word was *Mama* followed a day later by *Dada*. At ten months, "dogdogdog," a multiple dental, was easier for her than "Bo," the family dog. At fifteen months after six months in the "Baptist Pre-School of Hard Knocks," her vocabulary totaled seven words, and just three months later, it had swelled to thirty-five. At thirty-six months, she shows no signs of slowing. Though she cannot read, she thinks she can. Often, she will crawl into her sponge-rubber Bumbo seat with her favorite book (currently Disney's version of "Cinderella") and "read": "Yada, yada, yada, Cinderbella, yada, bad cat, yada, Lucifer, yada, yada, yada." Her first sentence had all the economy and force of Mickey Spillane: addressing the family Labrador, who cleans up any spilled food, she said, "No, Bo! My cheese." When she noticed a scratch on Omi's hand, she tenderly said, "Booboo, me kiss." Sitting on the deck blowing soap bubbles, I was ordered, "Get that bubble!" As she approaches her twenty-eighth month, she jokes with her father, telling him to "go to timeout," refers to her juice as her "coffee," and riffs on Spencer's name: "Bacci," "Baccho," "Baccho-Bacci...." As "Mommy" has succumbed to "Mom," and "Omi" to "Ohm," I'm jealous because I have yet to be christened by Lena's magical tongue.

Just as birds never learn their breed's song if their ears are plugged during the twenty-five-day window of opportunity, so are children vulnerable. The famed Hart-Risley study completed in 1995 has demonstrated in spades the importance of verbal stimulation. Unfortunately, radio, television, and "no, no, no" don't count. If children don't hear empathetic words, they won't learn language. By the age of four, children from welfare families have heard thirty-five million fewer words than their financially better-off peers. The result is a child who for all intents and purposes can never catch up no matter how diligent his teachers might be. Henry Robin thought all children needed a lap, but they also need lots of loving voices.

666: Numbers

Take *pi* out several million places, and you'll find eight consecutive eights. Or square 111,111,111 and find 12,345,678,987,654,321. Now I'd call those eights serendipity and the seventeen-digit "elephant on roller skates" the numerical equivalents of beauty, but many say it's God's way of saying, "Hello, I'm shy but real." Though Pythagoras never found those messages that we know of, he was convinced that, "All things are number." When I take into account the natural hyperbole of ecstasy, I think I understand where this Philosopher King was coming from. When I look at the "spiral nebula" in a pineapple or chambered nautilus, I confess to spontaneous emotion akin to religious awe. I feel like the supplicant on his knees, the ancient hieroglyph for a million, that Egyptians called "a man in astonishment."

Before there was a lodestone compass, travelers used the Big Dipper and Polaris to find their way home. If the night was clear, sea-borne wanderers could get their bearings by locating the dipper and following the lip of the cup to the pole star. With that reference point, the compass rose surely blossomed in the minds of many a lost sailor. I don't imagine it would have been difficult to persuade such a person that seven is a lucky number because there are seven stars in the dipper, one of the most recognizable features in the night sky of the northern hemisphere. Yet the realist in me says, "Study the dipper with a good pair of field glasses today, and suddenly the void between the dipper's lip and Polaris sparkles with so many stars invisible to the naked eye that finding north becomes far more difficult." There's a good reason man does not see with the hawk's acuity.

Apropos of nothing, my neo-Calvinist sister has told me, a pantheistic humanist, that I am destined for that Godless void she calls hell. I'm reasonably sure my condemnation has nothing to do with the fact that I live 666 feet above sea level. There are several churches and a university at the same altitude, and I don't see them worrying. Nevertheless, I confess to being fascinated with Revelation's "six hundred, three score, and six" which if written DCLXVI requires the first six letters in the Roman numeral "alphabet" in reverse order.

"What are we to make of that?" you ask. Absolutely nothing. Indeed one clan of Israelites returning from Babylonian exile numbered 666, and Solomon was paid 666 talents in gold every year, yet they weren't branded Satan worshipers. Like Freud's cigar, sometimes a number is just a number. Yet John of Patmos thought 666 portentous: in what I call a nightmare and others call a mystical vision, he read the number on the back of the beast slouching toward Bethlehem. I wish it were as simple as lifting a number off a jersey, for some Greek scholars think 666 is a mistranslation of 616. Instead, Christians numerologists have had to tie themselves in knots to make a name "mean" 666. The process is called "beasting," and for close to 2000 years, the number obsessed have tortured names to fit their Procrustean bed. The first place the fateful number was found was in "Nero" followed by "Diocletian," not surprising since both were ruthless persecutors of Christians. But many years later, some Protestants found the number in one of the pope's titles. Title, name, it doesn't matter; if you can't find the beast in Latin, try Hebrew. The Roman Catholics returned the favor by locating 666 in Martin Luther's name *if* one spells it "Martin Lauter." Lutherans still get a chuckle out of that one.

The trouble is that once the beast started slouching it proved to be relentless. Triple boxcars show up centuries later in Napoleon, Hitler, Stalin, Bill Gates, and Ronald Wilson Reagan's names. (How did good Southern Baptist Jimmy Carter miss that last one: three names with six letters each. It might have swung the election.)

But just who is this Satan? As soon as one generation identifies him, he morphs into someone else. My favorite contemporary sighting of the beast is that purple dinosaur on public television. Imagine my surprise when our grandsons' favorite dinosaur showed up in some fundamentalist Internet rants. It seems that if all three *u*'s in the phrase "cute purple dinosaur" are made *V*'s worth five points each, and one extracts and adds the Roman "numerals" *C, L, I*, and *D*, Barney is the Anti-Christ. I reassured our one grandson old enough to understand that if the phrase is "nice lavender lizard" or "adorable brontosaurus," the accusation fails. But it succeeds in any phrase using three *V*'s (or an *X* and a *V*), a *c, l, i*, and *d* in any order.

In 1994, when Snoopy complained to Charlie Brown that he had more 6's in a round of golf than the Book of Revelation, I thought the worst had passed. My spirits were lifted further when I read that the Bible-belt cough syrup "666" is celebrating its one hundredth anniversary in 2009. But as John Allen Paulos has ably demonstrated, we live in an age of innumeracy, meaning we don't know "ground zero" and "square one" from the navels we study. We make books like *The Bible Code* bestsellers because they "prove the divine authorship of the Bible." Well I admire "the good book" as much as anyone, but just because "Elohim," a Hebrew synonym for God, shows up 147 times in a very arbitrary computer search doesn't make me admire it any more than I already do. I'd just like to remind those who find exotic mathematical cryptograms in the Bible that the author of First Kings figured *pi* was 3.0.

Finding God's name in a blizzard of letters smacks of forecasting fortunes based on anagrams in one's name. I ran "Skip Eisiminger" through an anagram search engine and discovered that "I skimp the IRS genie." Well half of Washington may be skimping the IRS genie, but I never consciously have. Indeed, the IRS once sent me a note saying I had sent them too much, pointed out where I'd made my mistake, and included a check for $100! If you're like Samuel Johnson, you may be suspicious of that round number, as well you should be—it was actually $105.17. When a tax accountant re-ran the numbers for me the following year, she got a still higher number. Except for the speed of light and absolute zero, perhaps nothing should be chiseled in stone. *Pi,* for instance, is recalculated a little more precisely by each generation, and this is as it should be.

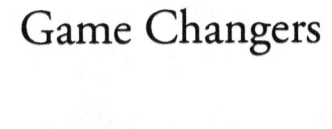

Game Changers

Game Changers: Change

"Fearsome chess masters fear the fearlessness of Deep Fritz."
—The Wordspinner

"Roll over Beethoven, dig these rhythm and blues."
—Chuck Berry

Several bad calls in the 2010 World Cup sent tremors through the soccer world. Sepp Blatter, the Luddite president of FIFA, soccer's governing agency, at first claimed the blown calls were reflections of the game's human element, and he feared relinquishing control to cameras. Metaphorically, Blatter is averse to placing rubber tires on a horse, but in truth, all that most fans want is to take the blinders off that nag before he goes to the glue factory. Before the Cup was emptied, however, Blatter said he would reconsider instant replays. We can only hope and blow loudly on our vuvuzelas.

Fear of the latest technology is often assumed without proof of harm. While it's true that industrial robots have killed several people working around them, the fault in most cases was the human's. And while robots were building robots as early as the 1980s, HAL isn't wearing the pants just yet. For one thing, radical change is expensive. I recall that one reason I pushed my father's hand mower for so many summers was the cost of a power mower. Yet every twig the size of a straw would bring the reeling blades of that misbegotten antique to a halt.

It's true, as the Italian proverb states, that, "Those born round are unlikely to die square," but I'm not talking about paradigm shifts. To return to soccer for a moment, I'm only advocating using the replays from cameras already in place in the major stadiums of the world. For those worried about the proverbial flow of "the beautiful game," I'd grant each coach three appeals, but if an appeal were upheld, it would not be counted against a team's total. The time taken to review the calls could be included in the stoppage time already added to each game. In most cases, the delays would total less than two minutes.

In addition to fear and costs, a vested stake is another reason people are reluctant to change. In Blatter's case, yielding to technology would be a tiny abdication of his control. A personal stake in most anything leads to a hardening of the arterial ways as illustrated by the "South-Indian Monkey Trap." To catch a monkey, Robert Pirsig says, simply drill three holes in a coconut: two for the chain, which is run through the nut and then locked around a tree, and a third hole for the monkey. This hole should be just big enough for the monkey's open paw to enter but not exit. The monkey's escape is thwarted because he usually has made a fist that cannot be withdrawn without releasing the fruit. Monkey values are so rigid that many allow themselves to be captured rather than surrender food. Like the monkey, Blatter has his fist in a very plump coconut, and he's reluctant to release that which he feels he's entitled to.

A joke circa 2005 posits an elderly man walking into Office Depot and asking the adolescent clerk for a Smith-Corona replacement ribbon. "I'm sorry, sir," said the youth after reflecting for a moment, "We don't handle ribbons, guns, *or* beer." I don't suppose one can blame the clerk any more than you could have blamed me if someone pushing a Model T had come to the Amoco station I worked at in the 1960s and asked for a hand crank. Twenty years later, I was not the first to welcome computers to the department where I was employed, but I wasn't the last either. One of my colleagues has never taken the computer the university gave him out of the box. I'm not sure if he drinks Pabst Blue Ribbon or packs a Smith & Wesson, but I know he still writes on a typewriter using ribbons his daughter purchases on eBay.

Opponents of reform often invoke the deity saying change would desecrate the holy order. Nineteenth-century writers from Thoreau to Baudelaire thought the steam engine was "the negation of God." Yet thousands today pine for a return of the glory days "when steam was king." They charter restored coal-fired locomotives to pull a few cars along a deserted piece of track before pushing the party home. Few, however, are willing to speak of the soot that the passengers breathe and wipe from their eyes. Of course, there's a place for these behemoths: it's called the Smithsonian, "the nation's attic." And judging from the massive "repentagon" a few miles from where I write, God has not been harmed by the railroads. In fact trains pass within a hundred yards of the place several times a day.

Like heartsick proponents of antique railroads, the Amish are famous for their resistance to technological change though a hundred years ago they did compromise by allowing seamstresses to use steel pins and needles instead of bone. Though you won't find any Amish overalls equipped with zippers, they have recently permitted the use of cell phones in an emergency.

Nothing makes my point better than an Amish farmer using a cell phone to call 911. This usage may be revolutionary in a culture that still plows with horses, but it's simply a more efficient way to handle complex events as they unfold. The latest technology, however, does not have all the answers. After buying my latest computer, I had to learn how to leave the first page of an essay unnumbered when writing in Microsoft Word. With

MS Office 2003, it took four clicks; with MS Office 2010, it takes ten. Both procedures accomplish the same thing, but the new way takes almost three times as long. While there are advantages overall to the newer system, I just wish there were some way to eliminate the "pain" of being on the cutting edge. But when I think I'll skip the latest innovation, I usually find myself becoming irrelevant.

Finally, back to soccer, where I began this rambling screed: FIFA is averse to adding instant replays because as one traditionalist stated, "Pelé did not benefit from that technology." That rationale is what G. K. Chesterton called "the democracy of the dead," or in Pelé's case, "the democracy of the retired." Pastured off as I am, I respect the deceased as much as anyone, but should they have a veto over something they never witnessed?

And while we're making changes, let's lower the pitching mound, widen the goal mouth, and raise the basket.

HOMO HARDWARUS: TOOLS

"But lo! Men have become the tools of their tools."
—Henry David Thoreau

"Man is a Tool-using Animal....Nowhere do you find him without Tools; without Tools he is nothing, with Tools he is all."
—Thomas Carlyle

With a surname meaning "mixer of iron" or "iron monger," I'm afraid that hand tools have been clattering along the Eisimingers' arteries for at least eight hundred years. As the proud owner of an awl and tack hammer purchased by my grandfather, and a bow saw and plane purchased by my father-in-law, the clatter of tools in my basement continues noisily apace. My grandfather Floyd was a railroad man but built much of his home. My German father-in-law Otto was trained as a cabinet maker but spent more time repairing WW I biplanes in the Luftwaffe. As a "dam engineer," my father is responsible for among other things, the Green Peter Dam in Oregon. And ever since I took "Wood Shop" in the seventh grade, I have been enamored of most anything that extends the hand's grasp and the arm's reach. At sixteen, there was a brief digression into guns, but after I helped to build our first house, the tools clattered back to the forefront largely because now I had a basement shop. If you've ever fixed a bike flat on an apartment stoop, you'll appreciate how pleased with myself I'd become.

With a hammer and chisel in hand, I felt like George Orwell, the colonial cop, with his rifle, "a beautiful German thing with cross-hair sights": Orwell had to shoot an elephant; I had to build something. Indeed, tools like guns possess a momentum of their own, and I was swept along building extra shelves in every closet and cabinet of our home. Before I finished, I had added over two hundred and fifty feet of shelving to the sixty that the carpenters had installed.

Then there was the furniture: a bedside table and book shelf for the bedroom, desks for our daughter and me, another book shelf for our son, a handsome chestnut cabinet for the television, a fold-away extension for the breakfast bar, shelves for the garage, two closets for the basement, and drug cabinets for the bathrooms. A nineteenth-century American proverb states, "If your tools are ready, God will find you work." I can't say I had any epiphanies; I just saw a void and tried to fill it. And yes, my edges were sharp.

After buying a square from Brookstone, I started receiving their gorgeous color catalogues with planes and saws posed seductively amid fragrant wood shavings. Half-consciously, I'd circle several hundred dollars' worth of new tools, and my wife would toss the order form away before I could put postage on the envelope.

As the house voids filled, my lust cooled, and I turned my attention to the car. I'd been changing the oil and filter for years, and then Bill Koon taught me how to adjust the valves on our VW. At the place where we buy our tires, I asked the price of a torque wrench. The owner, an old friend, recognized the symptom immediately. He volunteered that he'd told the Snap-on Tool salesman to take his business elsewhere. "Why?" I wondered. "Snap-on makes some of the best automotive tools in the world."

"Precisely, but they're expensive," the shop owner said. "Your torque wrench runs about $500. At Sears, the wrench you *might* use twice a year comes in under $200." A few months ago, he said that he'd discovered his mechanics were heavily in debt to Snap-on and planning to go deeper. Unless he wanted three more children to feed and a couple of angry wives, he had to act, so he told the salesman to stop coming around unless he was called.

When I mentioned the shop owner's pro-activism to my father, he observed, "Even if you have a lot of tools, it's getting harder to fix anything. Manufacturers, I suspect, are hiding the working parts from people like us so we'll break things and buy new stuff."

"Well," I asked, "you still change your own oil and filter, don't you?"

"I haven't even opened the hood because under it lies another hood, and it's bolted down! When I bought my car, the salesman told me that model Mercedes doesn't have a dipstick, so I figured what's the point?"

I long for the days when I could do the maintenance on the toaster we received when we married and cars like my Model A Ford, which was almost thirty years old when I bought it and still ran like my grandmother's Singer. I never had a proper garage for that red-spoked jewel, but that didn't stop me from sanding all the original black off her sinuous body and repainting her. A friend who'd recently returned from taking a yoga class in Nepal put me in a nostalgic mood when he told me the following story. He was walking through a small village near the base of Mt. Everest when he saw three men preparing to slaughter a goat. My friend said he figured it was a religious ritual, but he was puzzled by the street-side location. After the goat's neck was cut, one of the Nepalese hoisted the carcass onto the engine of a fifties era Chevrolet. Mystified by the proceedings, the friend asked a man in the crowd what was going on. "The engine won't start," the stranger said, "and nothing frees up a sticky choke like a sacrificial goat." Unfortunately, the friend didn't stay around long enough to see if the animal's body heat and natural lubricants fixed the problem.

Where screwdrivers are scarce, it appears that goats are tools. When my mother-in-law snapped a knife in two, it immediately became a chisel or flathead screwdriver for her husband. When my wife, who'd inherited her father's keen sense of perpendicularity, ordered a computer through the university, she was alarmed to find a loose screw in the box her machine arrived in. She immediately went to the phone and called the school's help desk. An Indian graduate student introduced himself and asked with extreme politeness how he could be of assistance. Said my distraught wife, "I found a loose screw in the box my new Dell was shipped in."

"T'row it away," he said without ceremony.

"Throw it away," indeed, I muttered and took it to my old mayonnaise jar.

Today I turn more frequently to my dictionaries than my tools, but it's nice knowing that my chisels and saws are positioned on the plywood surrounding my bench just waiting for the order to charge down. I may joke that a coping saw is an epigram of survival, and Moses may have been serious about a ban on hewn stones for the altar, but NASA has lost $100,000 worth of tools in space, and to me they are the stars that show the way.

ANTICIPOSTALATE: THE POST

"Please, Mr. Postman, de-liver de-letter de-sooner de-better."
—Georgia Dobbins et al.

"Sir Thomas Beecham never opened a letter unless it smelled of money."
—Anonymous

In case you have not cracked it yet, my title is a neologism for the heightened emotional state preceding the footfall or engine frequency that is everywhere recognized. Imagine a young man waiting to hear from the governor on a matter of life and death. Unless his heart has already stopped, he would likely be anticipostalate. I find myself in this condition most days I walk to the mailbox or open my email inbox. Henry Thoreau thought my expectation was a sign my interior life was failing, but I side with Randall Jarrell who wrote, "The spirit killeth, but the letter giveth life."

Indeed, there *are* times when life comes folded in an envelope. My wife was eight when in late 1947 she and her family received a letter and two small photographs of her father who'd gone missing following the surrender of German forces in May of 1945. Friends thought he was likely dead, but not the family. As an unreported French POW, he'd been ripping logs into planks with a two-man handsaw and helping a wine grower in Bordeaux. Needless to say, the family had been anticipostalate for a long time. The only letter, telegram actually, to rival that was the news three years later the family had won the lottery. There had been no anticipostalation on that one; it just sailed in one day with a feather taped to the back.

Postal pessimists like Thoreau might wonder why some duck hunter had not shot that plumed dispatch, but the reality is that a very small percentage of letters end up *"ex post fucto."* Indeed, neither my wife nor I have ever lost anything in the mail, insured or otherwise. Consider this: a letter sent to "Ft. Ignorance, TX" was delivered to Ft. Bliss, and no one "went postal," which, incidentally, is a misnomer. Of course, items are sometimes lost in transit, but often the blame rests on the sender. Nearly two hundred million items are burned annually by the postal service because of indecipherable forwarding and return addresses.

When mistakes occur, corrections are often made and apologies issued. Occasionally my *New Yorker* arrives with a torn cover in a clear plastic envelope, but a preprinted card explains how machines don't always work the way they're supposed to. A few years ago, a friend of mine mailed a letter from Greenville, South Carolina to Dresden, Maine only to have it land in Dresden, Germany. When the German postmaster realized the mistake, he placed the letter in a second envelope and dispatched it to its proper destination in the US. The extra nine-thousand-mile journey was paid for by a government of fallible though not spiteful humans.

Just think of the logistics involved in visiting two hundred million mailboxes six days a week with everything from slug mail to escargot. Whether by foot, bicycle, truck, plane, rocket, or sled, 95% of all first-class mail arrives at its destination within a day or two. How many of us would transport an unsigned Christmas card from Bar Harbor to Honolulu for $.45? Indeed that cost is the lowest in the world, and it's one factor in keeping three hundred million people from Maine to Hawaii thinking, "I'm an American." The six calories of starch in every lickable US stamp (kosher for the 1% who are Jewish) is a major component in the adhesive any democracy requires. Moreover, for many smaller towns and even some larger ones, the post office has replaced the tavern as the social center. Indeed, I would argue that an affordable postal system is as vital to a political union as a common currency or language. If the price of a stamp depended on how far it was traveling, we could expect a lot less mail from Alaska and Hawaii, not to mention Texas, which might not be a bad thing.

One of Thomas Jefferson's biographers has reported that while the third president received about five thousand letters in his life, he wrote some eighteen thousand. Given that many he sent were lost or destroyed, the letters sent surpass the number received by a factor of four. In 2011, *Harper's* reported that President Obama gets eleven thousand letters each day from which his staff selects ten for him to read. Those containing explicit threats, plastic explosives, or anthrax spores are read by the Secret Service, but to a degree, even hate mail is protected speech.

When email came along in the 1980s, I was pleased to discover that I actually enjoyed writing personal letters. What I didn't like was the tedious business of finding a suitable envelope, running down that return address torn from an old letter that had slipped from the address book, finding a stamp of suitable value, or running the whole thing by the post office. I've heard historians mourn the loss of handwritten letters, but I know several people like myself who print out our most meaningful electronic exchanges. I then paste mine in a journal.

Judging by the vast amount of unopened mail Hemingway left, it's fair to say he would not have appreciated the rhythm of email—short, staccato phrases delivered in a timely fashion before the energy of the emotion dissipates. A few years ago, our daughter in Charlotte wrote to say our granddaughter had a cold.

I wrote back a quick get-well email and signed off "I<3U."

Anja replied, "I less than 3 you?????"

I replied, "No, it's 'I heart/love you.' Tilt your head to the left—the <3 looks like a heart."

Anja replied, "I love you too!"

Said her father, "But I loved you first."

Said his daughter, "But I love you MORE!"

From alpha to omega, salutation to valediction, few things compare to letters from friends and family—handwritten, typed, or pixilated. To me they are the rubbings taken from high and low-reliefs; soft clay pressed to the brain; the sculptured residue of the heart; shallow, ink-stained ruts; faint strokes and pulsating curls. I love to see the sunlight sliding into the mailbox illuminating a sky-blue envelope with a foreign stamp. Switzerland issued one once that smelled of chocolate. I know because mine is safely filed away. The scent has long since vanished, but barring a fire, the words will outlive me.

FROM TECHNOPHOBE TO ALPHA GEEK: COMPUTERS

"Hackito ergo sum."
—Anonymous

President Eisenhower: *"Is there a God?"*
Anonymous Computer: *"There is now."*

In 1946, The University of Pennsylvania's ENIAC computer, built for the U. S. Army, weighed thirty tons, cost $500,000, and occupied 680 square feet or one New York apartment. Completed too late to help the Manhattan Project, its first job was to calculate the internal dimensions and external consequences of the hydrogen bomb. Thirty years later, Ken Olson, president of Digital Equipment Corporation, wrote, "There is no reason for any individual to have a computer in their home." When I read that, I thought, "And there's no reason for the hydrogen bomb either."

In 1980, our former minister confessed that he and his wife were "technology atheists" because they did not "believe in those $1,000 paperweights." I wrote back that despite having the last brain furnished with vacuum tubes, I had to think computers would soon be a fact of life whether we kept the faith or not. All my friends in the sciences were telling me to prepare myself, but like most Liberal Artisans, I was reluctant to respond. In 1983, *Time* named the computer the "Machine of the Year" in lieu of the traditional "Man of the Year" or more recently "Person of the Year." Of course, Hitler and Stalin had once made *Time's* covers, so I wasn't sure whether the computer was named for the harm it posed or the good.

In 1987, the two-time Pulitzer Prize-winner John Updike gave in to the pressure and began using a word processor, but he did not buy a modem because, he said, he had all the "time-sucking distractions" he needed. I understood what he meant when a computer-averse colleague bought an electric typewriter with a ninety-five-page instruction manual, which struck me as a considerable distraction. Whatever happened to peppering a piece of onionskin so hard the *o's* fell out? Back in the 1960s with no manual at all, I had taught myself to hunt and peck well enough to write a letter home. Good men coming to the aid of their country, I decided, needed manual typewriters.

In an essay reprinted in *Harper's* in 1988, that mossback Wendell Berry admitted that he still wrote with pen and paper, which his wife transcribed on a typewriter, circa 1956. Somehow he reasoned that if he succumbed to the charms of a word processor, he'd have to jettison, not only his Royal, but "my wife, my critic, my closest reader, [and] my fellow worker." In my copy of Berry's essay, I scrawled a big red question mark next to that line under which I wrote, "If you're really serious, Wendell, why not write with a goose quill on birch bark?" Though I still had a sign on my office door reading, "Pothole on the Infobahn," my sympathies were shifting.

In March of 1991, I walked into my office one morning and found a brand-new Macintosh Classic sitting on my desk. I had known it was coming because the dean had declared the college was going "paperless," and with this device, all memoranda would be handled electronically. Shortly after my "free lunch" arrived, I saw a Macintosh ad that read, "You can spell check everything…to ensure letter-prefect clarity!" It was not a good omen, and the department seemed to be using more paper than ever printing emailed memos.

Nevertheless, I eventually unpacked the Mac Classic and found myself in a puzzlement. I decided that I needed more help, so I signed my wife and me up for some instruction offered by the school. The first night, five or six of us novices were sitting at a row of computers facing the instructor with a screen of his own. "Okay, let's get started," he said after we'd mastered the on-off switch. "Now type, 'Are you in?'" That's what my brain understood, but what he meant was, "R-U-N." Suddenly a yellow exclamation point popped up on my screen, with a message reading, "There has been an error transferring your mail. I said, pass, shhhh! Don't tell anyone…" I figured the ghost in the machine was angry with me, but it was just some mysterious jargon I have never unraveled.

After Ingrid and I became comfortable sending email and surfing some of the less daunting waves on the net, she started calling India and the Philippines for technical assistance. One day, she called about installing some virus protection, and a patient fellow in Mumbai told her, "Okay, now pull up your desktop." Ingrid, who'd been on the phone for over an hour, said, "I'm sorry, sir, I can't. My computer is sitting on it."

We both felt like cannibals dining with silver forks for several months, but eventually we acquired a taste for the new cuisine. After I realized I wasn't going to lose my written work if I made too many changes and that one can make a thousand turns in the net's labyrinth and never get lost, we fell in love with this technological miracle. Though I still feel like I'm drinking from a fire hose when I'm using Google, I love the access I have to millions of documents that I used to borrow on interlibrary loan. More than once, I have closed a session with "Peecee," as I call her, and kiss the lips of her screen.

In an interview reprinted in *Harper's* in September of 1996, Kurt Vonnegut said he'd never use a computer because typing a manuscript and walking it to an urban post office, what his wife considered "farting around," was so much fun. On his way, he typically spoke to his typist by cell phone, some neighbors in a queue at the local newsstand, the vendor with a jewel in her forehead, and the postal clerk on whom he had a crush. Even with Skype, computers will never take the place of face-to-face contact, and anyone who's taken an online course realizes that.

Nevertheless, poor Kurt never got a computer tan. He went to his grave in 2007 without tasting the pleasures of writing on a computer. I've been putting my thoughts online for twenty years now, and people write me from all over—a Hell's Angel who wanted to know why he should have to wear a helmet as I'd advocated, a member of the NRA hot about my position on taxing ammunition to reduce the number of gun fatalities, my Calvinist sister who questioned my belief in free will, and a student at Bob Jones University who doubted whether I'd been to the school just days after I'd returned. Best of all, my father, who lived a thousand miles away in south Florida, and whom I saw perhaps once a year, began using email in the late 1990s. I now have hundreds of his letters in a scrapbook that I would not have had without the computer. You need to know that Dad is a taciturn Midwesterner, but once he mastered the new technology, he wrote, "Lead me not into temptation, but deliver me some email." Though a computer carded me buying a six-pack of beer recently, my father's prayer is one I repeat every night. Like robots the world over, the BI-LO computer was just doing its job, while freeing humans for tasks that machines will never usurp—smiling and meaning it.

The Write Stuff: Cursive vs. Keyboard

"Writing by hand makes you more apt to hear the inner voice."
—John Updike

"Writing words by hand is a technology that's just too slow for our times and our minds."
—Anne Trubek

A graduate school professor convinced me that if I really wanted to understand Emily Dickinson's bedrock subtext, I had to read the loops and line-outs of her ur-text. There was just no substitute for the manuscript—the author's last known revision of her text, her final wish. For years, I dreamed of cracking her "punctuation code": the subtle implications of each dash depending on its angle, length, and width. But I never made it to Harvard's Houghton Library where the Holy Grail for Dickinson lovers is shelved.

To further explain the significance of handwritten documents and my feelings toward them, I need to back up a century or so to 1751 when seven of my kin landed at the Port of Philadelphia. I've long been proud of the fact that each signed his name in the ship's register while many of their German cotravelers to the New World made crude *X*'s. Of course, the seven men spelled their names four different ways, but that's beside the point.

When I showed my father a photocopy of the seven signatures, he was reminded of some African-American draftees in the engineer combat battalion he commanded in World War II. While many of these soldiers signed for their monthly pay with *X*'s, others had to be shown how to make an *X*, so Dad decreed seven additional weeks of basic training to teach his men the three *R*'s. He doubted that he could mold an effective fighting unit until they could read, write, and do some basic computations. After twenty weeks of basic, no one was writing Spenserian stanzas, but there were no more *X*'s on the pay vouchers either. More important, Dad says, the fact that every one of the 660 men in the 1698th ECB could read and write at some level had much to do with the fact that no one died in combat, which included crossing the Rhine under friendly fire and advancing across Germany to the Elbe River.

As significant as the hand-printed or cursive signature is, the instrument for making one's mark is not as important as how much and how often one writes. Because writing makes a writer, he or she is better off hunting and pecking a thousand emails than penning a handful of Palmer-perfect thank-you notes. In fact, I'd venture to say that if children only learned to keyboard and never learned to write cursively, neither the world's forests nor the kids would be at a serious disadvantage. I'm assuming among other things that some terrorist doesn't explode a nuclear device that fries all the hard drives and servers in the world. If that happens, we may well be looking for a pencil and explaining to our kids, "This pointy end is the cursor, this blunt end is the delete key, and your CPU's memory is whatever you can hold between your ears."

But to return to my ninety-five-year-old father: I recently arranged nearly two hundred of his printed emails in a scrapbook for our grandchildren. Before Dad had a computer, he seldom spoke of the wars he'd fought in and never that I can recall put pen to paper on the subject. But once he discovered email, the journalist locked in ice sallied forth. His production has slowed in the last couple of years, not because he's exhausted the wars, but because he cannot remember how to operate the machine. Nevertheless, the computer made my father a better writer as well as a vastly more prolific one. The same can be said for many friends and family that before 1990 we were lucky to receive Christmas cards from him with a name scrawled across the bottom.

While it's true that typed notes lack the warmth and individuality of handwritten ones, especially one written in soy ink on linen-content paper, I have reached the point where I wink and tell students that graphite causes lead poisoning. So do ballpoint pens with blue, green, or red ink. Frankly, my aging eyes would rather read a typed assignment than anything handwritten by a twenty-year old with steroid-enhanced thumbs. The Educational Testing Service has long known that legible papers receive higher marks than messy ones. Once all students start keyboarding their SAT essays, we can expect the scores to rise even higher on a level playing field.

For years I was convinced that handwriting was essential to memory. If I could not recall a name, I'd write it ten times as I spoke it aloud. My better students told me that they used the same technique studying for their exams. Something about the physical act of handwriting, they said, helped engrave information in the memory bank. Once I even tested my thesis by asking a class of twenty-two to write my wife's unusual maiden name ten times. Actually one third wrote "Barmwater" cursively, the second third printed it, and the control group just watched as I wrote it on the board for the others to copy. I then took up the papers saying nothing about why I was doing this. Five days later I asked all students to write my wife's name on a piece of scrap paper. In the cursive group one wrote "Barmwell," another wrote, "—water," and seven had no idea. In the print group, one wrote "Bramhammer," another wrote, "Bumwater," and eight had no idea. In the control group, one wrote "Bromwater," another wrote, "B—," and seven had no idea. The results were sadly inconclusive. I just wish there had been enough students with laptops present to see how they would have fared by typing the name.

Despite my love of the keyboard, I confess to feeling a compulsion to write on every steamed mirror I pass, but the future surely belongs to QWERTY. The French may keep their Bonapartes, the Germans their Friedrich Wilhelms, and we our John Hancocks, but the sooner we all switch, the sooner thirty-eight million letters will arrive annually at their proper destinations instead of the dead-letter office. The sooner thousands of taxpayers whose addresses no one can decipher will receive $95 million annually in refunds. And the sooner some 7,000 of us will stop dying annually as a result of illegible prescription orders.

Despite all the scribbling monks in the scriptoria of medieval Europe, there is nothing sacred about taking quill, pen, or pencil in hand. I will, of course, continue to write congratulatory and condolence letters by hand in ink, but just as the Irish monks devised Uncial to distinguish themselves from Roman Catholics, and English Puritans devised a script called Copperplate to distinguish themselves from Catholics, so should we not be afraid to change "fonts."

Personally, I'd continue to teach handwriting, but only as an elective after the fifth grade. Cursive is as quaint today as Coca-Cola's Spenserian script. But when was the last time you heard someone order a "Coca-Cola" instead of a "Coke"?

Bluetooth Headsets and Treadmill Desks: Multitasking

"If you're up to your butt in gators, you may have forgotten why you were draining the swamp."
—American proverb

"I'm not multitasking; I'm switch-tasking. There's a difference."
—Anonymous

Recently my wife drove over to Anderson to have her oil changed, and, hoping to kill two birds with one stone, she walked to Best Buy next door. At one of the stand-up desks, Ingrid spied a geeky fellow in tie and jeans busy at his keyboard, so she sidled up and waited for him to finish. When it was apparent that the employee had a great deal of typing to do, she cleared her throat and said, "Excuse me, I have a brief question."

Without looking up, the clerk said, "Keep talking; I'm a multitasker."

"OK, well, uh, an Apple-owner friend of mine cannot open the PowerPoint presentations I send her, and I was wondering what she could do about it."

"She'll have to buy the Apple PowerPoint app," he said without looking up. Indeed, he *never* looked up. Hurt by his glib, impersonal behavior, Ingrid asked to speak to the store manager.

"But he gave you the information you requested," the manager said. "Your friend will have to buy that app if she wants to open those presentations."

"I know, but your employee never stopped typing, nor did he once look at me!"

"Eye contact is not required of our associates, ma'am," he said looking away. "Accuracy is."

I suppose one could argue that asking a computer question while getting the oil changed is the equivalent of texting while dealing with a customer, but I would challenge the premise. I confess to sometimes listening to NPR while I shower, but that qualifies as multitasking only to the Amish. Imagine me dropping by a colleague's office to ask a favor. And say that in the middle of that conversation, I start another one with a passing book buyer. Most, I think, would say that I was being controlling and self-serving. Having been left dangling at my desk while more pressing business was conducted in the corridor, I know how it feels to be needed one minute and placed on hold the next.

Notice that I said *sometimes* I listen to the radio. Most of the time, I just sit in the shower and let hot water beat on my back—it's my one vice.

Call it multitasking, but I know that it's in bed, in the bathroom, or on the drive/walk to work that I get my best ideas, assuming I'm super-saturated from my prior reading and discussions. After a good night's sleep, not the guarantee it once was, connections often start to occur to me the way fireflies illuminate the dusk. Of course, they were flashing on and off before, but the contrast was so poor, I could not see them.

Were I to leave the radio on 24/7, I'm certain that would be the death of originality in me, and if I'm not original, why bother to write? A study done at Stanford in 2009 confirmed what I've suspected since our son claimed he was "studying" for his final examinations with AC-DC blasting from his stereo. The researchers revealed that productivity, attentiveness, and retention rates of multitaskers are impaired by watching television while reading. Moreover, people trying to do two or more things simultaneously miss subtleties that close reading and undivided attention bring.

It's hard to believe that Samuel Johnson, perhaps the finest critic produced in the eighteenth century, used "original" and "creative" as terms of derision. As late as 1939, one of Peter Ustinov's tutors at Westminster wrote that the boy "shows great originality, which must be curbed at all costs." What originates in the shower or a conversation for me is honed and polished alone in the quiet of the study. Add a cowriter, editor, or jangling telephone, and a writer can kiss opportunity goodbye. For most of us, creativity varies inversely with the number of pens using the same inkwell. I know that group brainstorming never worked for me, for "say something original" is as intimidating as "say something funny."

I recall a colleague finding me at the office one Sunday afternoon and inquiring if I had a "death wish." I said, "No, just a work lust." I wish I'd thought of it at the time, but as the proverb states, "One man's rut is another's groove." And regardless of the calendar, the groove is where I love to be especially since the age is looming when I will finally unplug my keyboard. So I struggle to be less busy in order to do more of the work I enjoy.

A year or so later, the same colleague who wondered if I had a death wish presented an English Hour lecture on rhetorical theory. Returning the favor she did me by attending one of my lectures, I attended more out of courtesy than any interest in theory. Over about thirty minutes, she read a densely reasoned essay all the while showing about forty slides of long quotations many of which, while pertinent, were not used in her essay. Frankly I was lost: should I read the material on the screen or listen to the speaker? After a few minutes, I decided to read because the quotations were more interesting than what I was hearing. When it was over, I asked her about the slides, saying the experience was similar to watching cable news where at times there are talking heads, stock quotes, ball scores, and the weather all crawling across the screen at once. "Does anyone expect a viewer to absorb all this data?" I asked. A younger colleague piped up in defense of the speaker, saying he and his wife often spend an evening using their computers with music in their earphones and two small televisions on their desks tuned to different stations. I sensed I was outnumbered and left thinking we are raising a generation of ADD victims.

Walking my bike through a crosswalk on the way home, I was nearly struck by a top-down convertible driven by a student. I yelled; he stopped and then quickly backed up. "Sorry, man," he said, "I was changing the CD." I waved him off and headed for the beer cooler.

I've told our children that I wish to be cremated, and one thing they can do with me then is to place a tablespoon of my ashes in an egg timer. If I end up also being used as a paper weight, I'll probably be grateful for the work but not before.

LET'S SEE WHAT DEVELOPS: PHOTOGRAPHY

"A new industry [photography] has arisen which contributes much to confirming stupidity in its faith and to ruining what might have remained of the divine in the French genius."
—Charles Baudelaire

"[Photographs] are magic things that traffic in mystery. They float on the surface, yet they have a strange life in the depths of the mind. They bear watching."
—Lance Morrow

Some claim that the Shroud of Turin is the world's first photograph created when a burst of light transfigured the body of Jesus and left his negative image on the linen. "Photograph," however, did not exist in any language until the early nineteenth century. In 1824, the French photographer Joseph Niépce called the new medium "heliography," or "writing with sunlight." A short time later in England, William Henry Fox Talbot coined "photogenic drawing," or, "a picture born of light." Then in 1839, Sir John Herschel used "photography," or, "writing with light," before the Royal Society, and it stuck.

As these word histories remind us, light is the catalyst in recording the visual whether it comes from the sun or burning magnesium, which in the early days not only illuminated the subject but sometimes ignited the photographer's hair. One of the interesting ironies in precipitating a picture with light is that it will last longer if it's kept in the dark.

The older I get, the less I wish to be circumscribed by a rectangle of time I don't recognize, and when I do, I don't like. Apparently, I'm not alone. At age ninety-nine, Sigmund Freud's mother complained that her pictures in the newspaper made her look a hundred. The Amish and some orthodox Jews refuse to be photographed at all because of the Bible's injunction against making "a likeness of anything" lest they or someone else make the mistake of worshipping these icons. No point in taking any chances, they say, regardless of how unphotogenic they might be. Some aboriginals refuse to be captured on film because the process strips the self of its natural protection. Anthropologists find that hard to argue against when they're holding the evidence in their hands.

Henri Cartier-Bresson, one of the finest photojournalists of the last century, said that the camera was "a combination of the psychiatrist's couch, a machine gun, and a warm kiss." On another occasion, he called the device "a Geiger counter." Permit me to borrow these four analogies as a rough outline for my further ramblings.

First, the psychiatrist's couch. When photography studios opened by the hundreds across Europe and America in the late nineteenth century, the first and often the only thing people wanted written in light was an image of themselves to pass along to their children and grandchildren. It's no wonder; few could afford an oil portrait or a copper engraving, and the silhouette was a simplified likeness in which almost everyone had a strong chin and a noble brow. With the camera though, immortality was democratized.

More to the psychological point, my sister once sent me a photograph that a stranger had taken of her family arrayed beside and across an armored personnel carrier. The four were visiting Ft. Jackson where the younger son had just graduated from basic training. Sadly at the time, my sister and her husband were tied up in some nasty divorce proceedings, but they had set aside their differences for that "Kodak moment." When I saw the photograph, it fell to this self-appointed photo-shrink to expand its meaning. At the risk of over-simplification, suffice it to say that my sister had her arms around her two boys on the APC while the estranged husband stood alone on the ground.

Second, a machine gun. If you doubt the roadhouse-right impact a photograph often has, take a look at Kevin Carter's famed picture of the starving Sudanese orphan in the fetal position being measured by a vulture. Cartier-Bresson surely had a picture like Carter's in mind when he made the gun-camera connection. Not long after Carter took his Pulitzer Prize-winning picture and shooed the bird away in tears, he committed suicide. The stiletto shaft of light that entered the aperture of his camera passed through the lens, the film, the metal case, and into his brain. Every time the picture was mentioned, he was reminded that he had spent twenty minutes framing the shot and neglecting to help the child to the refugee center.

Third, a warm kiss. Greta Garbo's film career began with a love affair, but as she aged, she said the camera had become a "predator." There's no question about the seductive and voyeuristic appeal of iconic film, whether moving or still. In Garbo's case, she often seemed more alive and tangible on the screen than she did dodging around New York in a kerchief and sun glasses trying to avoid the stalkerazzi. What she feared, I suspect, was something Sony introduced in 1998—a video camera equipped with a $7 infrared filter which peers through people's clothing.

Perhaps the ultimate "warm kiss" that a camera can bestow is what ecologists have dubbed "eco-porn." These are photographs of the Grand Tetons, for example, taken with "provocative lighting" that attempt to seduce the viewer into saving them at the expense of "flat-chested" landscapes.

Finally, the Geiger counter. Surely this figure addresses photography's ability to take the invisible measure of a subject. It's like a nurse taking your blood pressure and pronouncing your heart fit. Two examples come to mind: one is the photograph of a South Vietnamese general summarily executing a suspect on the streets of Saigon, and the other is of American soldiers and a Vietnamese girl fleeing down a country road, terrified by a napalm explosion that had burned her clothes off. Both of these pictures were taken and sent around the world in 1968, the year many historians say the majority of Americans quit supporting the war. Viet Nam was suddenly radioactive, and the camera more than anything else had documented the lethal ticking.

In praising photography, I'm forced to admit the shortcomings of my own preferred medium: writing. Frankly, there are some things words cannot imbue with agency. I grew up with a father who developed his own photographs and smoked three to four packs a day. My mother smoked a pack every couple of days. Until I left home at seventeen, I felt as if I were living in a Midas muffler—quiet and smoky. About 1967 near the time that the surgeon general issued his famed report on the hazards of smoking, *Life* published two full-page autopsy photographs. One was of a beefsteak-red lung belonging to a non-smoker, who'd died in an accident. The other was of a tar-black organ belonging to a smoker, who'd died of lung cancer. After seeing that juxtaposition, I was never seriously tempted to smoke again. Every time I'd sneak a few puffs off a stray butt left in an ashtray, that dead black lung would loom before me.

When my father saw the *Life* photographs, he weaned himself from a twenty-seven-year habit over one weekend. Today he's ninety-five and fit. Mother too quit, but it took her a few years to break the habit. She died at eighty-six. I'll let you draw your own conclusions regarding smoking, but without question, photography packs a wallop—just ask a portrait painter if you can find one.

Thinking Outside the Bachs: Musical Instruments

"Charles II slept through the sermon, but woke for Westminster's great pipes."
—The Wordspinner

"I got a fever, and the only prescription is more cow bells."
—Christopher Walken

In the sixth grade, I took violin from the band director at a public school in Falls Church, Virginia. If only I'd appreciated what a rich opportunity I'd been given, but I blew it off like Satan when offered a chance at redemption. Mozart and Beethoven meant nothing to me, so I faked it for the entire year. Knowing I'd never have to solo for the teacher, I played "air violin" in the school orchestra rather than contribute to the "noise" around me. I just had to be sure to sit behind this girl who took music as seriously as I took baseball. I plagiarized her bowing, forged the fingering, and no one, including my proud parents, was any the wiser.

Six years later as a high school senior, I fell in love with the tropical music of Xavier Cugat and Martin Denny, especially the bongos in the rhythm sections. One day I took some of the money I'd made delivering newspapers and biked into town to a pawn shop I'd seen ads for in the paper. I bought a cheap set of bongos, pulled up a chair, crossed my legs, and began drumming. However, with a blacksmith's ear for music, I wore my fingers raw making minimal progress at best.

The two paragraphs above constitute my confession that I have no performance expertise, but ignorance has never stopped a writer. Since I have taught some music history in humanities courses, I know a modest amount about the development of musical instrumentation, and I have some rather strong opinions, both borrowed and original. The time has come to air the grievances.

I'll start with a handful of sound-producing implements I have never heard, but whose strident names (unlike the didgeridoo and fiddle-de-doo) are not promising. These include the rackett, the aquaggaswack, and the clackamore. Moreover, I have no desire to download Chopin played on an "Excedrin thumb piano," but I admire the maker's honesty. Though women claim size does not matter, the three-and-a-half-acre stalacpipe organ and the nanoguitar are ludicrous judged solely on their bulk or lack thereof. Call me biased. Then there's the German Überorgan, which produces impotence in those who make the mistake of thinking about it. Finally, I exclude the cheese drum, the beer-bottle organ, and the cigar-box guitar from my band or orchestra because they stink of the garbage they were salvaged from.

Moving to the more conventional instruments, here are a few of my favorites:

• Sir Malcolm Beecham thought the harpsichord sounded like "two skeletons copulating on a tin roof."

• The British radio personality Irene Thomas claimed the cello has "a lugubrious sound like someone reading a will."

• Anonymous thought the harp looks like a piano that's been hung up to drain after the hunt and doesn't sound much better.

• Anonymous also thought the viola's range is about thirty-five yards if one has a good arm.

• The oboe is "an ill wind that no one blows any good."

• The bassoon is "a clarinet with strep." I would only add that it surely must be a major cause of apoplexy in the performers.

• And the double bass usually "sounds best in the trunk of a taxi." The latter opinion was expressed by a friend who had tired of wrestling his bass onto Gotham's buses and subways.

At Carnegie Hall in 1924, George Antheil cornered the market on rude and raucous "instruments" in a work called *Ballet mécanique.* Think of a cole slaw grater on your knuckles, and you'll get the idea. Taking the lead from Mahler who'd used cow bells in his sixth symphony, and Tchaikovsky who'd called for cannon in the *1812 Overture,* Antheil scored his work for player pianos, automobile horns, an airplane engine, a tam-tam, a set of electric bells, and a siren. Remarkably, not a single human shared the stage with the appliances during the performance. Soon, the auditorium began to clear, led by a gentleman who'd tied a white handkerchief to the tip of his umbrella. I understand that he and his followers were directed into a POW compound in the lobby until the robots concluded their hammering. Had I been in attendance that evening, I would have followed that flag in search of a tune that did not draw blood to the porches of my ears, carrying a sign reading, "Give me melody, or give me death."

My grandmother used to love the Lawrence Welk Show, and I was often required to watch with her to "improve" myself at a time in my life when there was no improving on Elvis and Fats Domino. Listening to Myron Floren and his pleated box, I came to hate the accordion and concertina on those nights of enforced culture. Gary Larson captured the way I felt in one of his cartoons: "Welcome to hell," says Satan to some new recruits, "here's your accordion." Satan might have added, "And here's the music to 'Lady of Spain.'" Then one night years later, I was watching Austin City Limits when Clifton Chenier and his Red Hots appeared playing "Bon Ton Roulet." Thanks to this "swamp pop" zydeco band, in less than an hour, I had forgiven the squeeze box for all the suffering it had wrought.

I had a similar conversion experience with the skirl of the bagpipes. In college, my friends and I shared jokes about mistaking the "doodlesack" for haggis or the Geneva Convention banning it outright. Then watching the funeral service for the firemen killed on 9-11, I understood what Ervin Lewis meant, "Blood should be stirred before it is spilled, and nothing does it better than bagpipes."

Since I grew up in a family that revered "the Bourgeois Trinity" of Mantovani, Percy Faith, and Lawrence Welk, it should come as no surprise that I never heard bluegrass until I was in college. The banjo was another one of those instruments I had learned to hate by never listening to it. Then I heard Earl "Mephisto" Scruggs playing in "Foggy Mountain Breakdown," and I understood the mojo that bluegrass performers invoke by gluing rattlesnake rattles in the pungent hollows of their instruments.

Friedrich Nietzsche, who believed life was a mistake without music, apparently never heard the "jumping flea," better known as the ukulele. The instrument, in my unstable opinion, makes death by fleas appealing, but then I've never been to Hawaii either. Stay tuned; I may get there yet and change my mind.

IN THE TEETH OF THE WIND

A few days after graduation,
after they'd trued their rims,
highlighted their highways,
circled their daily goals,
and packed their panniers,
Shane and his friend, Mike,
rode their dream westward
toward that fuzzy gray dot
where the shoulders merge.
They said they'd write when they got there,
but Maude produced a book of stamps
and thrust it down a pant's pocket.

On a brisk, cloudless day,
they agreed Skip could ride
the first leg with them.
Though the wind swallowed
his valediction,
the hand at their back was welcome.
Without a truck in sight,
he flirted with going the distance.
At the crossroads though,
Skip stood and waved
as two blue helmets
dropped below the horizon,
into "*Mare Incognita*,"
where the old maps said,
"Here be dragons."
Then he turned and recrossed
the blurred terrain wiping tears
on the loose ends of his sleeve—
must have been the wind.

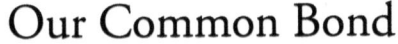

Our Common Bond

FROM SOOT TO DIAMONDS: ORDER

"Behind all agreement lies something amiss,
All seeming accord cloaks a lurking abyss."
—Albert Einstein

"I believe in Spinoza's God, who reveals himself in the orderly harmony
of what exists."
—Albert Einstein

I still hear my Mother saying: "Skippa, would you finish the squash? It's in a bowl I have to wash."

"By whose order, Mother?" I said impertinently.

Seven decades later when she was incapable of doing the dishes or the laundry, Dad took over and established a schedule, "On Tuesdays, I do the towels," he wrote me, "on Saturdays, I do the sheets…"

By that time I knew who'd issued the order.

When I started dating the German woman who would become my wife two years later, I thought I'd found some respite. That notion held up until her mother secretly laundered my London Fog raincoat ("Dry Clean Only") and shrank the poor thing two sizes. She felt terrible, of course, and said she'd make it up to me by roasting a chicken for Sunday dinner. As we ate, I was relieved to see that my girlfriend and I processed the bones about the same. Then I looked over at my mother-in-law's plate and saw a neat pile resembling the sundried phalanges of a Capuchin ossuary.

Both my mother and mother-in-law had survived the Great Depression, and I've often heard them use the 1930s as a scapegoat for their curious disorders. But I've also known others in and out of the family who came through the thirties unscathed. I swear one survivor I know could swallow scrap iron and excrete a coil of haywire.

Haywire, as it turns out, has an interesting reputation: coiled neatly on a spool in the feed-and-seed store, it's still haywire, but most of us especially the nonfarmers among us think of it as a rusty rat's nest. But the truth is, haywire around a bale of hay creates an orderly and manageable solid that can be heaved into a hayloft without breaking. More interesting to me is that while the wire is doing its work wrapped around a confusion of hay, the chaos is pushing back preventing its restraints from "going haywire." Thus chaos creates order and vice versa.

I was born in 1941, so I cannot blame my "rage for order" on the Depression. I'm a clean-desk man, certifiably neat, who orders the same thing every time he enters a McDonald's or an Olive Garden. Unlike my grandchildren, I enjoy stacking up blocks more than knocking them over. I line up my coins by value as I prepare to buy something from a vending machine, and I shuffle the cards at least seven times to insure a random mix. Chinese food often leaves me hungry probably because I miss the salad-salty-sweet pattern of a Western meal. (Let's face it; a fortune cookie is a poor substitute for a slice of cherry cheese cake.) And when I used to play golf, I was sure every birdie would be followed by a bogey though bogeys usually pointed to double bogeys, not birdies, down the course.

In the twelfth century, *Tau-Omega* maps depicted the Mediterranean as a straight, horizontal line with the Nile descending like a culvert from the middle of the sea on a planet resembling a giant hockey puck suspended in space. Framing the known world and the T (*tau*), which trisected it into continents, was the perfect circle (*omega*) of the ocean. Though I cannot imagine Odysseus finding his way home with such a map, it is charming to moderns, cleaning up the Middle East as it does. Equally attractive are a spotless sun, an uncratered moon, circular orbits for the planets, and crystalline spheres to hold them all in place. Johannes Kepler was so disappointed with his discovery of elliptical orbits that he spent ten years trying to refute himself. I know the feeling: once I received that first "B" in college, I knew there was no way I'd ever be 4.0 again.

I also recall reading of a warden who refused to alphabetize the list of one celebrity inmate's four hundred authorized visitors. The frustrated prisoner, whose guests had been denied entrance when the gate guard could not locate a name, volunteered to organize the list. The warden denied the prisoner this opportunity because the guests, he said, were "not going to come in alphabetical order." True enough, yet in a world where bedlam is often cubed, the Giant's Causeway in Northern Ireland is formed of 40,000 deftly interlocking basalt pillars. Moreover, plucked guitar strings form perfect sine waves; snow stops falling at -30 degrees Fahrenheit, and everything from the chambered nautilus to the Helix Nebula appears to have been designed by a Fibonacci mathematician.

I'm not sure one can infer a benevolent god from this evidence, but he, she, it, or they seem to have the same appreciation for order that I have. Or so it seems. If nature is governed by some ineffable imperative, how does one account for the floods, tornados, and asteroids that occasionally punctuate the harmony of a sunny day when the daffodils are in bloom? The answer seems to lie in attribution: my idea of order does not always coincide with nature's. While the golfer is cursing the lightning that seared his arm off while shaking his putter at a dark cloud, the farmer across the road is counting his blessings knowing that the same bolt fixed some nitrogen in his soil.

My first impression of Leonardo's drawing of "Vitruvian Man," squared and circled, was that he can also be framed by an equilateral triangle. Once posed to perfection, however, he may think he's "the paragon of animals" since no other beast fits those forms the way he does. I know that salt crystals are born as perfect cubes, but I also know that while seven planets orbit the sun counter the clock, Venus thumbs her nose and spins merrily along in a clockwise direction. Moreover, every zebra mother has a different stripe pattern, every Emperor penguin its own call, and every dog has a unique smell. These infinities don't cause confusion; they prevent it.

The Primal Shrug: Nature's Indifference and the Church

"Honor the Lord with thy substance, and with the first fruits of all thine increase: so shall thy barns be filled with plenty, and thy presses shall burst out with new wine."
—Proverbs 3: 9–10

"Between 1753 and 1786, 103 French sextons were electrocuted pulling their rain-soaked bell ropes in an effort to disperse lightning."
—The Wordspinner

The gods are larky tonight," says one aboriginal to another as both are struck by cream pies from heaven. Starting in the 1950s, as best I can judge, *The New Yorker* started publishing a series of cartoons by several hands showing an often nearsighted god standing at the edge of a cloud and throwing down the kitchen sink, the garbage, chocolate bars, a sheaf of lawsuits, and plain vanilla lightning. In the eighties, He grows lazy and uses a TV remote. As the nineties dawns, He's sitting at a computer observing some urban schmuck. As the victim walks under a piano being hoisted to a penthouse, God reaches for the key labeled, "Smite."

Recently, He was shunted to the disabled list when His doctor declared He was out for the season with a torn rotator cuff. But He's evidently come back strong: in the last year or so, the Black Saturday bush fires have torched the Melbourne area, an earthquake in Haiti has brought an entire country to its knees, a volcano in Iceland stopped air traffic in Europe, and that hole in the Gulf spewed a half million tons of crude oil before it was plugged. I know, BP caused that last one, but if God really cares about us, He could have pinched off that hole with one small seismic shudder. For heaven's sake, the pipe was seven inches in diameter.

As one who has long been in the position of trying to explain John Dryden, Alexander Pope, and Ben Franklin's claim that "Whatever is, is just," I try to stay current on how God treats his creation, especially His church. Let me review the last couple of centuries: on All Saints Day of 1755, the Lisbon earthquake shook down several churches, a convent, a hospital, and a cathedral. This uppercut was followed by a neat one-two combination: a tsunami and a conflagration, all of which left around 50,000 dead or about as many Americans who died in Vietnam. In the deity's inscrutable way, He left more brothels standing than houses of worship. In 1760, a confidently ungrounded Venetian church volunteered to store the city's gun powder in its crypt. Seven years later, it was struck by lightning, killing some 3,000 residents in the area. In 1886 the Very

Reverend Dr. J. B. Kavanagh of Kildare, Ireland was killed when a stone cherub in the ceiling of his church broke off and struck him in the head. In the earthquake and subsequent fires of 1906, many San Franciscans noted the irony of allowing Hotaling's whiskey warehouse to stand while many of the city's churches fell or burned or both.

Now imagine a steeple impaling a sanctuary roof in a Florida hurricane, the National Cathedral losing three of the four pinnacles on the central tower in an earthquake, several dead refugees who'd sought asylum from a tornado in an Alabama church, and a Louisiana place of worship with three inches of mud on the floor after a flood. Finally, consider the two-year old who drowned playing in a baptismal font and the minister electrocuted during a baptism when his microphone fell in the water.

Most of these stories came from the *Greenville News,* which does a poor job covering world events, so if you're thinking God is anti-Christian, I suggest going through the files of a major paper in Beijing, Cairo, or Mumbai. A brief search I made turned up the following: in the hajj of 2006, at least 360 pilgrims were "crushed in a stampede to throw pebbles at Satan." And one pilgrim from Pakistan was swallowed by a shifting sand dune. His body has never been found. Judging from the evidence, I'd say the church has about as much clout with the Almighty as gnats, maybe less because from where I sit, it seems the gnats are winning.

After the Lisbon quake mentioned above, one British vicar startled his congregation by arguing that the massive loss of life was a sign of the Almighty's mercy because Portugal deserved far worse: its armies had slaughtered uncounted thousands in colonizing the New World. Perhaps so; I'm in no position to judge the compassion of shifting tectonic plates and a tsunami fifty feet tall, but why wait until 1755 when the conquistadors were exterminating innocents as early as 1505?

Matthew actually got it right about 70 AD when he observed that the rain falls on the just and unjust, but the church has largely ignored this simple fact and metaphor. It seems that after every flood there's one preacher who concludes the disaster was not a bad thing but a generous foretaste of the apocalypse. This clever argument turns the recent devastation into something good for the believers and bad for the doubters. Nineteenth-century scientists, most of whom were faithful members of one church or another, said God's benevolence lurked in every horror. One could not call the deity malevolent, they argued, if He opened a door for each He shut. Thus obliterated homes are a trifling inconvenience compared to the fertile mud every flood brings, and the deaths caused by lightning are compensated by the twelve pounds of nitrogen that thunder storms annually bestow on every acre. I don't know about you, gentle reader, but if lightning killed one of our grandchildren, no amount of fertilizer would assuage my broken heart.

Darwin's faith in benevolence, what was left of it after his daughter died at age ten, was quashed while studying the wasps. One species, he discovered to his disappointment, paralyzes and lays its eggs in caterpillars in order that the wasp grubs will have a living larder as long as they need it. It's a bit like a human infant hatching inside its mother's breast, feeding at will, and bursting out at age twenty-one with all the education it will ever need. The only moral Darwin could draw from parasitism was the neutrality of nature, for life, it seems, is like a lump of copper ore exposed in a landslide. Heated briefly to twice the temperature of the sun when struck by lightning, the ore bleeds molten copper, but cooling in the wind and rain, it soon begins to oxidize.

Life most likely began in a similar way. The right ingredients and forces were in the right place at the right time. It just happened. We could not help ourselves. Was God stirring the pot or nature? I'll let you decide.

The French poet Paul Valéry argued that God made everything from a void, but "sometimes the void shows through." I recall reading of an English fox hunt to which several of the royals were invited. It was such a splendidly pompous occasion with lots of red coats and polished tack that the local vicar was asked to bless the proceedings before the fox was released. While all heads were bowed, the hounds meandered about the freshly mown field, and one urinated on the only vertical structure in sight: the vicar's starched, white robe. The dog knew better than to void itself on a horse's leg. At any rate, the void came shining through. It usually does.

THE CHARM OF THREES: THE TRINITY

"I tell you the solemn truth, that the doctrine of the Trinity is not so difficult to accept for a working proposition as anyone of the axioms of physics."
—Henry Brooks Adams

"Oh, I takes de gospel whenever it's pos'ble..."
—Ira Gershwin

The French essayist Montaigne speculated in the sixteenth century that "if triangles invented a god, they'd make him three-sided." Guess what? They already had in the fourth century at the Council of Nicea, just twelve years after Constantine had legalized Christianity. At the emperor's behest, church bishops met to confront the threat of the "Arian heresy," the belief that God's son is not of one substance with his father. Though Jesus had told his disciples to baptize "in the name of the Father, Son, and Holy Spirit," and two of the patriarchs had written about various triads, "the Holy Trinity" was not an integral part of church doctrine until 325. The beauty of the concept allowed Christians to attract monotheistic Jews to the faith while retaining the divinity of Jesus and his shadowy companion, the "holy ghost." By the 11th century, however, a dispute over one word in the Nicean Creed led to the great East-West split that culminated in the formation of the Roman Catholic and Orthodox churches. *Filioque* ("and from the son") was the word that divided them, and the issue was whether the Holy Spirit "proceeds" from God alone (the Orthodox view) or from God and his son (the Roman view). One patriarch was so incensed by the implied demotion of God that he excommunicated the pope, which led the pope to excommunicate the patriarch.

To attract converts and explain the concept to their illiterate followers, Christian artists began experimenting with a variety of ways to symbolize the Trinity. Perhaps the earliest device involved three interlocking circles à la Ballantine Beer. Abstract as the circles were, it satisfied the precept that two of the threesome were always invisible to man. Gradually, however, a hand or eye in the sky came to represent God before He became a bearded old man in a robe. The dove had been a convenient stand-in for the Holy Spirit ever since Noah, and the son was represented by a cross, a book, or a lamb before he was shown as a boy seated on his mother's lap. When some South American artists used a three-headed man to represent the Trinity, Pope Urban VIII in 1628 forbade its use because he felt it promoted polytheism. The great mathematician and physicist Isaac Newton thought that belief in the Trinity was a violation of the first commandment—worship no other gods but Jehovah; nevertheless, three fish, hares, eagles, lions, or tendrils on a triangular grapevine were deemed acceptable. Church officials frequently alluded to the Trinity in their gestures (the three-fingered blessing of the right hand), their dress (the Pope's three-tiered tiara), and church architecture (the trefoil window to name just one). All of which in the nineteenth century led William Ellery Channing to declare, "We [Unitarians] are astonished, that any man can read the New Testament, and avoid the conviction, that the Father alone is God."

From earliest recorded times, the triad has been a popular moralistic and mnemonic device. In an effort to explain unity amid diversity and offer an escape from head-butting dualisms, priests and teachers of all stripes turned to the smallest number that can represent this universal intellectual need even at the risk of oversimplification. Familiar triads include: a human consists of mind, body, and spirit. The French march under the banner of liberty, equality, and fraternity. Matter exists as gas, liquid, and solid. Theology concerns itself with heaven, earth, and hell. The personality splits along the ego, superego, and id. Nature is animal, vegetable, or mineral. Time is past, present, or future, and speeches should have a beginning, middle, and end. Idioms and proverbs often use triads such as, "Three's a charm"; a drunk is "three sheets in the wind;" and every genie grants its liberator "three wishes." Long before the Bible, there were Osiris, Isis, and Horus in Egypt; Odin, Thor, and Frigg in Scandinavia; Anu, Ea, and Bel in Sumer; Brahma, Vishnu, and Shiva in India, and Zeus, Poseidon, and Hades in Greece. By the first century, the authors of the New Testament understood the convenience of triads, and so we have "faith, hope, and charity," three Magi, three Marys, three denials of Peter, three crosses on Cavalry, and three days of Jesus's death.

In his 2007 film documentary, *Religulous,* Bill Maher interviewed one fellow dumbstruck by the power of three. The young man plays Jesus at an Orlando theme park that featured presentations of his passion six days a week. Apparently "Jesus" had given a lot of thought to his role because he used a clever analogy for the Trinity that took the celebrity atheist by surprise. The Trinity is like water, the actor said; it exists in three states, solid, liquid, and gas, yet it's always fundamentally H_2O. Back in the van, Maher confessed that the analogy was "brilliant," but ultimately "bullshit because it proves nothing." Well, no, analogies are not properly proofs or even arguments; they are approximations of complexities best used in expositions. So I have to side with "Jesus" on that one. I just wish Maher had given the actor enough time to explain his analogy—is God ice because He is the solid foundation of the Trinity, or water because He's necessary to all life, or gas because pantheistically He pervades all nature?

A quick check of Google uncovered a weedy abundance of what Rudyard Kipling called the "tangled trinities." St. Patrick explained the mysterious triad using a shamrock: it's like three leaves growing from a common stem. Others have explained it as an egg consisting of shell, yolk, and albumin; a coin with two faces and a rim; a candle with three wicks; a football snapper, holder, and kicker; three dimensions in space: length, width, and height; a government with executive, legislative, and judicial powers; a parent who's simultaneously father, husband, and son; or a can of "3-in-One-Oil that cleans, lubricates, and prevents rust."

In 2006, the conservative journalist Cal Thomas was annoyed with the Presbyterian Church (USA) when it voted to consider a policy paper that merely suggested replacing "Father, Son, and Holy Ghost" in the liturgy with among other things, "Mother, Child, and Womb." Indeed, how can there be a holy Trinity, I have often wondered, without a feminine component? Would a "Quaternity" be so bad? I doubt that the proposal will ever leave the committee's table, but had I written it, I would have cited one more alternative, Robert Ingersoll's trinity of science: "Reason, Observation, and Experience."

Imaginary Friends: Divine Humor

"Absence of evidence is not evidence of absence."
—Carl Sagan

"Tornadoes prove that God's a drive-by killer."
—Anonymous

Some call it the Promised Land; others regard it as a Harp Convention. But somewhere off in the wild blue yonder, there's an ornamental wrought-iron fence with signs reading, "Beware of the god," and, "Cubs fans, wait here." At the gate sits a bearded man in wire-rim glasses holding a quill pen. Two large keys dangle from his belt while two shallow boxes, one marked "Save" the other "Shit List," clutter the desk. It is soon apparent that the gate-tenders (variously a black woman with an Afro, a heavy smoker, and a homosexual) do not accept bribes. Inside the gates, the spoken language is Aramaic, neutered dogs find their testicles restored, and molting angels lie about in a swirl of loose feathers wishing they'd brought something to read. At the center is a hole in the ozone, and overhead, as if seen through a glass darkly, a host of celebrities gaze from their skyboxes.

The composite I've sketched above comes from a lifetime of jokes and cartoons: everything from G. O. D.'s trucks ("Guaranteed Overnight Delivery") to erudite analyses of Billy Graham's 1,600 square-mile "Kingdom come." If the right reverend is correct, the saved will spend eternity sitting around a fireplace waited on by angels or going to parties in "yellow Cadillac convertibles" on streets paved with gold. As a Democrat and secular humanist, I question Graham's use of heavenly resources when so many terrestrials could use an IRA.

God-satirists do not have to travel far for material especially since Google has given everyone with an iPhone access to everything from Washington's Library of Congress to Tokyo's National Diet Library. A friend of my father's, who was stationed in Japan on the first of January 1946, listened in amazement to Emperor Shōwa (Hirohito) as he told his Shinto adherents via radio that he was not, as he had previously claimed, a god. While he *had* entered a large sphere and waited for the sun to rise on December 25, 1926, as his spokesman later claimed, he had *not* been transformed into a woman, copulated with a male deity, and been reborn from his own womb as a male. American occupation troops snickered under their breath while the Japanese mourned the death of another god. Most deities like Baal and Isis just retire to the crosswords.

From the outsiders' perspective, all religions are comic, which leads them to wonder, "Who makes this stuff up?" In the case above, I suspect ancient Shinto priests, who perhaps felt that the more tortured the common sense, the more sustainable the credibility. Virgin births, walking on water, raising the dead, and a host of other hyperbolic occurrences kept my friends and me chuckling through our adolescence as we scoured illustrated texts searching for God's anthropomorphized navel, Adam's uncircumcised penis, and Abraham's "bosom."

The Christian and Jewish deity has over seven hundred names and nicknames, not counting modern slang references like "Gee," "Gad," "Gosh," "Jerkhovah," "the Infinite Orgasm," "the Cosmic Bellhop," and "God All-Smitey." Most of these later terms have no attribution, but given their extra-Biblical appearance, I assume they have human pedigrees. When it comes to the deity, humans are a lot like a dog sniffing a sealed can of Alpo. Our exquisitely tuned senses tell us He's in there, but our paws cannot operate the can opener.

It is, of course, human nature to poke fun at what we do not believe. Having created a hell on Earth, as George Steiner observed, we refuse to believe that it exists elsewhere. Indeed, in 2007, Pope Benedict declared that Limbo is no longer in limbo; it is history. Could purgatory be next? I could have saved the Vatican cardinals a lot of trouble, for any belief insisting that undying pain is the punishment for questioning everlasting love is destined to fail.

John Kane's captionless zinger was on the mark when he drew Adam, à la Michelangelo, reaching for the Creator's hand, but what our ancestor cannot see is an electric buzzer, which the almighty clown has palmed. Kane's vision should remind us that the earthquake that leveled San Francisco, including most of its churches ("Bazinga!"), left Hotaling's Distillery standing. That was in 1906, but in 2005 following Hurricane Katrina, some God-inspired wag posted this sign on a church, "God welcomes His victims." As I have written elsewhere, "Even if you're black-clad orthodox, God sometimes sends you the chicken pox." And as my father used to say, "Amen, goddamn it!"

Nevertheless, though love is my currency, the invisible clockmaker still winds the sundial in the backyard. Though some may think of Him as remote, perhaps they haven't heard his patter on a tin roof. Through a foggy silence comes a voice, and somehow I know a nod from a shake. So, whether you are Christian, Muslim, or Jew, the God in me greets the God in you. No joke.

RELUCTANT TO WALK ONE STEP AHEAD: COMPETITION

"From a worthy opponent great wisdom flows."
—*Confucius*

"Before you try to keep up with the Joneses, be sure they're not trying to keep up with you."
—*Erma Bombeck*

Though competition originally meant "seek together," it still brings out the best but also the worst in us. I recall reading about Lance Armstrong slogging his way up some impossible Alpine road when some French women stepped from the crowd and spat on him. I imagine it had something to do with rumors that he was cheating and those t-shirts and bumper stickers that read, "America 6, France 0." To level the playing field, a few American women raised their blouses and bared their breasts when their blue-eyed boy passed. Lance said it felt like a tailwind, and he continued cheating to win his seventh Tour in seven years.

New Yorker cartoonists despise the desperately competitive perhaps because their profession forces them to vie weekly for places in the magazine that publishes them. Barbara Smaller has one monk in training say to a fellow disciple, "When I was making money, I made the most money, and now that I'm spiritual, I'm the most spiritual." Victoria Roberts draws a woman saying to her tennis opponent, "I'll be the headlights, you be the deer." And Robert Mankoff invents a man on a couch telling someone on the phone, "You're depressed? My depression makes your depression look like euphoria."

"Once competitive," I've heard critics warn, "always insatiable." In the 1990s, the still hungry "Peanuts" billionaire Charles Schulz threatened to kill Charlie's beagle if Lynn Johnston, creator of "For Better or Worse," allowed her beloved but aging sheepdog to die. Schulz was furious that a dead Farley might receive more publicity than Snoopy.

In our normal-for-the-most-part family, we compete in all manner of ways including playing "burn-out" with a Frisbee, holding our breath under water, and eating hot peppers. A few years before she died, my mother had a pre-dinner conversation with her pastor's mother, which I eaves-dropped on while setting the table with the pastor. Mother opened by saying, "My daughter in Arizona has a college degree in home economics but is doing very well in real estate."

"That's nice," the guest parried. "My son in Florida has a degree in physics and teaches middle-school science."

"Well, my younger daughter in New Jersey has her MA and leads self-discovery workshops."

"My son in North Carolina has degrees in biology and geology and teaches high school in Charlotte."

"Our son Skipper has a Ph. D. from USC and teaches at Clemson."

"Our daughter and your minister has her Doctor of Divinity degree from Duke." Mother was stumped—she had no more children and no more degrees, divine or otherwise. Before the two could get into the grandchildren, Dad announced that supper was served.

Dad is also competitive, but he is his own worst opponent. When he was eighty-one, he set his mind on shooting his age on the golf course. After a tournament at his club, he emailed me the following, "I came as close to shooting 81 today as I'll ever come. The score keeper told me after the 17th hole that I needed a par five on 18 to reach my goal. I hit a good drive, a good lay up to the creek, a decent chip shot to the fringes of the green, and a second chip shot to within six feet of the hole. I then two-putted for an 82! Our team came in first, but that wasn't much consolation." My father, I must say, is the sorest winner in the family.

My sisters have several dogs in the hunt as well. The older is so theologically competitive that she has informed her sister, now an ordained minister, and me, a missionary humanist, that we are both going to hell because her faith trumps ours, but that's grist for another mill.

Forty years before our Methodist minister went to the seminary, she was spending the night with two of her cousins. Before going to sleep, my sister suggested they all pray beside their beds. The first cousin prayed for a minute and hopped into bed. The second prayed for another minute before she quit, but my sister stayed down for an estimated ten minutes. Years later, one cousin told me how impressed she'd been with my sister's devotion. When I relayed that to the minister, she admitted she'd stayed on her knees as long as she had largely to impress them. "I would have stayed longer," she said, "but I was kneeling on a hardwood floor."

I told her not to feel bad, for I had competed in similar petty ways. Once when Dad was eighty-four and I was sixty, Dad came to visit. While I was urinating, I heard him in the guest bathroom starting to whiz. I tried my best, but even though Dad got a late start, he finished first. This craziness appears to be inherited because often when I shake hands with one of our grandsons, he says, "One, two, three, four—I declare a thumb war."

Years ago, when a friend asked why I was so serious about my running, I replied, "So that somewhere, sometime, I can beat someone." But in recent years, the pilot light in my competitive furnace has begun to flicker. Often, I'm like the first guy in this old joke. A rich guy approaches another rich guy at their exclusive club and asks if he might catch a ride home be-cause his Rolls is in the shop. On the way home, the first leans over and innocently asks, "What's that."

"The tachometer."

"Okay and what's that?"

"The light indicating I need an oil change—say," the driver said, "I thought you'd ridden in a Rolls before?"

"I have but never in the front seat."

Subtlety is the name of competition at my age. One night when my wife finished brushing and flossing her teeth before I did, I laid her flannel nightie out in the guest bedroom. I jest, of course, but if winning is the sac-charine on the wedding cake, and losing is the toothpick the baker forgot, I think I'll have some fruit. I don't like beating someone, nor do I like to lose, so I Frisbee with my wife, and as we toss, we schmooze.

One or Two Degrees of Separation: Celebrity by Proxy

"The celebrity is a person who is known for his well-knownness."
—Daniel Boorstin

"I was lucky enough to marry a girl who had been bitten by one of [Faulkner's] dogs."
—Robert Canzoneri

When an old poker buddy of mine was a sophomore in college, he telephoned T. S. Eliot's home in London. Barry Hannah, later nominated for the National Book Award, just wanted to tell the poet how much he'd admired "The Love Song of J. Alfred Prufrock." Although Eliot was having his calls screened, Barry did get through to the great man's valet, who promised to convey the acknowledgments and salutations "at the very earliest convenience." Barry left his number, adding that Eliot could reverse the charges, but he never returned the call.

Often that's the way it is with celebrities: they percolate up through the folk, but when they're charging four bucks a cup, they're too good to return a call. For several years, I have been using the same gym as a local novelist with a well-deserved national reputation. One afternoon, I entered the weight room to sign in and noticed that the attendant was reading the novelist's latest. I asked the young man how he liked it, and he said, "It's great!" I said I had enjoyed it as well and then went to my daily flogging. As I was mounting my machine, the celebrated writer walked by without looking up and headed for the exit. I've known him since his student days, but I was willing to give him the benefit of the doubt—he just didn't see me. After all, I had not seen him until he was almost past. As the belt began to turn beneath my feet, I watched the novelist leave right past the attendant without so much as a "see ya." When I left, I asked him if he knew the author of his book. "Oh, sure, he was here a short while ago," he said.

"So you met him here?"

"Oh, no, he lives right up the street from us; he's my best friend's father!" The departure without acknowledgment didn't seem to bother the writer's star-struck admirer; indeed, the approximation of fame is often sufficient for the unfamous. I know it is for me.

I was primed for my role as a back-row fan by my mother. When I was just a few months old, Mother waved and held me up for President Roosevelt to see as we were strolling on Duke Street in Alexandria, Virginia. After all, she always maintained that I was the prettiest of her babies, so she was not surprised when the president waved back. Now this was April or

May of 1942, and FDR had a lot on his mind at the start of a two-fronted war, but he was generous enough to wave back.

When I reached the ninth grade in Columbus, Georgia and began to develop a sense of what "famous" really meant, I was delighted that my English teacher had also taught Carson McCullers. A few years after moving back to Northern Virginia, I found myself carrying the newspaper of the commercial artist who drew the famed Coppertone ad: the dog pulling down the swimsuit of the little girl on the beach. When I was old enough to drive into DC, I took my girlfriend to among others a Harry Belafonte concert in Rock Creek Park. In college, I ordered a book from Vanderbilt on interlibrary loan and discovered that the check-out card had been signed by Randall Jarrell, Allan Tate, and John Crowe Ransom. Since the libraries were shifting to computer cards, I slipped the worn memento into my pocket. Until now, no one has ever been the wiser.

When Burt Lancaster came to town in 1973 to film *The Midnight Man,* my wife and I went up to the Clemson House one evening to dine. As luck would have it, the person before me in the cafeteria line was, you guessed it. Burt ordered the roast beef, and I ordered the same, so I could tell my grandchildren that I ate a slice of meat whose "twin" was eaten by one of Hollywood's greats. It wasn't exactly a laying on of the hands, but no piece of roast beef has held more significance for me. I've also derived some vicarious satisfaction from holding a baseball signed by Babe Ruth, riding my bicycle on some of the hills Lance Armstrong battled in the Tour de Trump, catching a whiff of Shawn Weatherly's perfume before she became Miss Universe, and listening to Bishop Tutu bless our two children at their graduation from the University of South Carolina.

While the amps vary, there's no question that celebrities generate voltage. After shaking hands with a Roman Catholic priest, I realized that I had intruded in the line begun by Jesus' apostles. Though history has taken no notice of my handshake, the apostolic succession I've joined is empowering. My friend John Butler, who directed the Tiger Marching Band before retiring, once visited the White House after playing the Clemson-Marland football game. Since John shook JFK's hand, and I've often shaken John's hand, there is some unspoken but palpable connection to a man I admire like standing next to Beethoven's piano or handling one of Emily Dickinson's manuscripts.

I suppose the closest I've been to a celebrity for any extended time was the year I spent in four classes taught by the poet, critic, and novelist James Dickey. I owe Mr. Dickey a great deal; after all, he directed my dissertation. But most celebrities, I've learned, are very busy people, and that's the reason they keep their heads down when there's nothing to be gained by engaging in small talk with a weight-room attendant even if he is a neighbor. But busy or not, one thing I cannot forgive Dickey for is distributing unsigned poems in class and pretending they were the work of students. "Hey," the defender argues, "Mr. Dickey needed some feedback, and he didn't have time to read a bunch of lousy student poems."

"But," I say, "for five hours a week, he's paid to teach, not wax his résumé."

Moreover, as soon as one of the "birds" in his singing nest made a name for himself, Dickey was quick to claim him as a writer he'd feathered. Every Wizard of Oz, it seems, is one-part hokum.

But back to the family: my reverend sister, who has meditated with the Dalai Lama, reminds me that our Mother fed Cary Grant a deviled egg at a post-war picnic in Heidelberg, Germany. Our daughter wiped up some of Michael Jordan's sweat from the floor during a nationally broadcast game. My wife once watched the future NFL star William "The Refrigerator" Perry eat a large box of Cheerios, walk outside the dining hall, and dunk a basketball. "It was," she said, "a beautiful moment." And many years ago, I gave a D to a future presidential candidate.

But there are more profound dangers to fame: take Luciano Pavarotti. At the conclusion of one performance, he took 165 curtain calls over sixty-seven minutes. The problem, of course, is that Pavarotti thought he deserved 165 curtain calls and a clown car full of roses.

A Tune to H₂O: Water

"I never drink water because of the disgusting things fish do in it."
—W.C. Fields

"I've taken a proprietary interest in our children and Lake Hartwell for over forty years."
—The Wordspinner

In *Wind, Sand, and Stars,* Antoine de Saint-Exupéry writes of three Moorish chieftains who had never drunk from a sweet-water spring. Prior to 1930, the three had lived in the Sahara all their lives and had dug in the sand for most of the urine-scented water they'd ever drunk. Then a mail pilot in the service of the French diplomatic corps flew them over the Atlas Mountains and the Mediterranean to France where they saw green pastures, cows with udders near the bursting point, trees taller than a dune, and roaring cataracts all for the first time. As they stood awestruck by the aquamarine abundance of the French Alps, their guide begged them to leave, but one chief said he wanted to wait until Allah shut off the tap. The puzzled guide assured him that these falls had roared for thousands of years and would continue to do so long after they left.

When the chiefs returned to the desert, they broke into tears telling about the trees and cows, but they kept the blue torrent to themselves lest the faith of their followers in Allah be shaken. "The God of the French," one said privately, "is more generous than the God of the Moors."

The gods who open and close the spigots of heaven are indeed fickle. One small hill town in India receives 467 inches of rain each year while some places in Antarctica, which harbors 70% of Earth's fresh water, have not had a fresh flake in a million years. Yet stone harpoon heads have been unearthed in Saharan caves. Closer to home, Lake Hartwell, which is about three miles from where I sit, was twenty-two feet below what the Corps of Engineers considers "full" in November of 2008. Local mayors found themselves invoking mandatory cutbacks on people accustomed to hydrotherapeutic extravagance. Just a year later, the lake with a coastline of nearly a thousand miles was up twenty-four feet.

Because Americans are so blessed (the country averages about 45 inches of precipitation per year), we typically use seventy times more water than Ugandans do and four times more than the Swiss, where the depth of Alpine glaciers is measured in miles. Only in America can one still find toilets that use three and a half gallons of drinking water to flush away a cup of urine. Comprising just 5% of the Earth's population, Americans account for 20% of its waste in all forms. Only in the States, where a couple of generations back people took weekly two-minute "horse baths" *if* they needed one, do people take half-hour-long showers. My German wife has scolded me for forty years to shorten my ablutions, and I have: they now average fifteen minutes, but it's unlikely that number will shrink anymore because I enjoy shaving while hot water bathes my sore back. I am learning; it only took me a decade to get in the habit of turning off the water while brushing my teeth.

One place you won't find me indulging myself is at a California-style water bar choosing among two-hundred brands of bottled water including Russian Orthodox "holy water." Has no one noticed that "evian" spelled backward is "naïve"? Call me cheap, but I refuse to pay more for water than I do regular gasoline. When carcinogens turned up in Perrier in 1993, I thought the scam would wither and die, but stories of nanotraces of hormones and antibiotics in tap water had people scared. Never mind that most water is distributed under more stringent guidelines than the stuff packaged in bottles made from 17,000,000 barrels of oil per year. Often bottled water *is* tap water as PepsiCo acknowledged in 2007 when they agreed to add the words "public water source" to every label of Aquafina. Other bottlers are cannier arguing that they aren't selling water; it's "portable hydration." Where is the child among us who will stand up and say, "The Emperor is a con man; it's all H_2O"?

The latest riff on selling oil to the Arabs is bottled holy water. One brand called Holy Drinking Water is blessed *en masse* in the warehouse by an approved Anglican or Catholic priest. Another brand, Spiritual Water, offers ten scenes from the Bible to choose among while deciding which bottle you want to buy from a former pest controller. And Liquid OM, according to the bottler, gives the purchaser cosmic energy. Of course it does—every bottle is immersed in a "gong bath" before leaving the plant. My plasma is rebooted just writing about it.

That which should be cheap and abundant to all is the stuff of natural science, but it often reads like myth. Without "the universal solvent," the Blue Ridge Mountains that I can see from my window would be taller than the Himalayas—30,000 feet, instead of the three to four thousand they are. By the same token, Niagara Falls will be as flat as a Mississippi sandbar in just 23,000 years. Moreover, a single gallon of water yields a cubic mile of fog. And ice under 600,000 psi will not melt in boiling water, nor will it float.

One of the beauties of water is that no matter how contaminated it becomes, it can always be filtered and aerated until clean. A drop of rain that falls at the headwaters of the Thames may be safely drunk and excreted eight times before it reaches the sea. And just a few years ago, veterinarians successfully replaced lost blood in mammals with—you guessed it, sea water.

Should humans ever manage to contaminate water absolutely, there's plenty of the virginal variety in space. We now have solid or liquid proof of water on the moon. There's an excellent chance that it also exists on Mars as well as some of Jupiter's moons, and the Orion constellation features clouds that dump a volume of water greater than sixty of all our oceans combined every day.

How are we going to retrieve that water, you ask. Well, it seems that we already take delivery of close to two million tons from the Aquarian realm every day. Over the next 20,000 years, this perpetual cosmic hailstorm will produce another inch of water for the entire planet. And at the current rate of global warming, the seas are expected to rise over two hundred feet in this millennium. Where I live at 666 feet above sea level, this increase will not give my future neighbors a beach-front home, but it will make a trip to the coast two to three hours shorter.

As my semi-lavish showers suggest, I love water. I drink at least sixty-four ounces daily, swim in it every opportunity I have, and play in it with the grandchildren until I emerge shriveled as a dried peach. Moreover, my Calvinist conscience insists that I'm not really exercising unless I'm sweating profusely. Unlike many I know, sweat does not offend me, especially my own. On a humid day in South Carolina, you'd better like your greasy secretions, or you're going to be very unhappy living at this Moroccan latitude. Working or just walking among the tall, skinny pines of August, water trumps champagne, and it won't leave you with a headache either.

Synergy: Our Common Bond

"Nothing human is alien to me."
—Terrence

"As the Apple is pulled down, the Earth is pulled up."
—The Wordspinner

Though surely inevitable, the strain created by a black president in The White House is beginning to show, so it's time to remind ourselves what we have in common, and that globalization doesn't necessarily mean Americanization.

With 205 national teams competing in the 2012 Olympics, nearly seven billion humans had a team to applaud. When Yao Ming plays in Houston, three hundred million Chinese turn on their televisions to watch American basketball, potentially quadrupling the size of the audience. If Yao turns an ankle, however, the global economy shudders.

If you're looking for globalism in sport, FIFA, which organizes soccer's World Cup, boasts 208 member countries. As for political representation, 192 countries are currently enrolled in the United Nations, giving over six billion of us access to the world's ear. Should the Grand Master of the Sovereign Military Order of Malta (population three) ever address the General Assembly, UNTV will surely broadcast the speech. Though his or her Excellency may address the council in Italian, the audience, which speaks some 6,800 languages and dialects, can listen to a simultaneous translation in English, the closest thing to a universal language the world has ever enjoyed. Thanks to the spread of English, someone will know at least, *OK, hotel, bar, sex, cool, weekend, stop, jeans, no problem, telephone, Coke, hamburger, and Marlboro.* Isn't it a comfort to know that if you have a few dollars you can order a meal, a drink, a bed, a prostitute, and a smoke wherever you are?

If you take the time to ask your foreign hosts about their color preferences, you'll learn that the vast majority of us prefer pink over yellow. If you hear infants learning to speak on your travels, you may notice that they learn their vowels before the consonants. We all master the labial and dental sounds before tackling the velars and gutturals. If someone tells you of a nightmare in which he was naked and unprepared for a test, you'll understand because you've had the same dream.

Moreover, someone in the vicinity will be able to play chess with you, and most will understand your facial expressions and body cues, win or lose. Though they were not grown or made outside South and Central

America until the sixteenth century, tomatoes, potatoes, and chocolate are sure to be found close by. If it's not too cold, there's a good chance the people you see on the streets will be dressed in T-shirts, flip-flops, and jeans. If they're laughing, you'll recognize the pattern: a sudden explosion of syllables (*heh, ho, he,* etc.) each a fifteenth of a second long, repeated four or five times per second.

If you're a physician, scientist, or engineer, the Indo-Arabic language of science and mathematics will serve you well, for it has long been universal. Of course, the symptoms for everything from malaria to AIDS are recognized by doctors of every stripe. All carbon-based chemists know Mendeleev's table of elements, and every physicist is conversant with the laws of thermodynamics.

If you've brought your children with you, they will find their native peers enjoying "hide and seek" and jumping rope as much as they do. Some may chant rhymes that you learned as a child half a globe away. Should you need a break, 140 countries celebrate Earth Day every April 22nd. Should war break out, we can take some comfort in the fact that for sixty years now every nation has promised to abide by the Geneva Conventions.

Should you desire to worship with your new neighbors, you will discover that their Golden Rule is the same as yours—not just a rule, but the most esteemed rule of all. If you stay for any length of time, you'll also discover that your neighbors believe that actions speak louder than words, giving is better than receiving, elders are to be respected if they've earned it, no one lives solely by what they put in their mouths, and the truth will make us free.

If you are a cultured person, abstract art speaks a universal language, which is why abstractions are so common in ecumenical houses of worship like the UN chapel in New York, the Rothko Chapel in Houston, and St. Henry's Chapel in Turku, Finland. If music is more to your liking, a major third elicits "joy" wherever that note is played while a minor third is "tragic." As for composers, the world's musicians play Mozart more frequently than any other because his orchestral work is the closest anyone has ever come to "absolute music," music without a trace of nationalism. Even when lesser talents like Michael Jackson die, the world mourns, and a man in Macau spends $420,000 to buy the singer's rhinestone glove.

If we really want to be fundamental in our search for a common bond, we should know that we're all constructed of atoms recycled from long dead plants, animals, and stars. The life expectancy of an atom is ten (years) followed by thirty-five zeroes. A mere 13.7 (years) followed by eight zeroes is the time that's passed since the Big Bang, so we can stop worrying about immortality. In one form or another, we're going to be around for a very long time. Of course, every one of us is related to a small band of Africans who left the continent of our birth about 60,000 years ago, which makes us all *Homo sapiens sapiens* whose DNA is 99.9999% identical. Furthermore, every time we drink a glass of water, we can be sure that at least one of those H_2O molecules passed through Jesus, Mohammed, or Buddha, and with every breath we take, there's an excellent chance that some of those nitrogen atoms passed through Hitler, Stalin, or Mao. But neither the good nor the bad will ever leave its mark on "our" water and air. Without the diphtheria, smallpox, rabies, and polio medicines developed by German, English, French, and American doctors respectively, our lifespans would be about thirty years. In 2012, the world's average was sixty-seven, the longest it's ever been. And, only six to nine individuals separate us from every other person on the globe.

Just as thirty-four countries pooled their resources in 1990 to expel Saddam Hussein from Kuwait, so would the armies of the globe rise to fight an alien invader that wished us harm. Given a common foe, the petty differences of melanin concentrations, hair sections, and nose widths would fade to insignificance. In addition, if James Lovelock and Lynn Margulis's "Gaia Hypothesis" is correct, the entire earth and every natural thing on it is one "living, self-regulating organism." Whether we have hemoglobin or chlorophyll in our vessels, we all have a common goal: the dissemination of DNA in the universe. For when the God(s) of your choice said, "Go forth and multiply," He, She, It, or They did not place any spatial limits on our fecundity. He…just pointed us into space.

May the force be with us.

People Are Our Teachers

Gatsby Redux: Romantic Fools

"No amount of fire or freshness can challenge what a man will store up in his ghostly heart."
—F. Scott Fitzgerald, *The Great Gatsby*

"Rekindling a former flame may be a cold enterprise."
—The Wordspinner

Because of the advantages I had enjoyed by virtue of birth, my parents, like Nick Carraway's father, advised me to suspend judgment as often as possible. But since Gary's upbringing and opportunities were equivalent to my own, I'm going to drop the pretenses; like Jay Gatsby, my old friend was a bright fool.

Gary and I were army buddies in the early 1960s, but we went separate ways after mustering out. In June of 2000, I had not written or spoken to him in almost forty years, but while writing my Cold War memoirs for the children, I realized there were a number of details I'd forgotten. A quick Google search, however, located his telephone number for me. To my pleasant surprise, Gary seemed to have a sound-and-sight-recording camera built into his ganglia.

Though he recalled that the German woman I married worked at the *Staatsbank,* I remembered Gary only as a nearsighted, solitary soul who wore black civvies the way Gatsby wore pink suits. He was so enamored of our electronic espionage work that he dressed monochromatically and wore dark glasses in the dense fogs of Northern Europe. In my second or third email to him, I wrote, "Give me the names of any German friends, and between Ingrid and me, we should be able to get some news while we are there in July." My wife and I were planning a trip to see her family near the site where Gary and I served in the shadow of the Iron Curtain.

A few days later, Gary wrote, "There are some people in Helmstedt that I would like to get updates on. Please let me know the latest I might e-mail you before you leave. If I could ever decide how to handle it, there is a personal issue that has been out there for thirty-eight years and still hasn't scabbed over." The day before Ingrid and I departed, Gary sent us the name of Elke Guttenbach. She was the "personal issue" that was still "out there." "While we were dating," he confessed, "I wore a suit of armor, and she wore a magnet."

A few phone calls in Helmstedt supplied Ingrid with Elke's phone number and address now in Berlin, a two-hour drive east. When he learned that Ingrid had found his "Daisy Fay," he responded, "It is 4 in the morning, and I've been sitting here with your e-mails in my hand for seven hours just trying to sort everything out. The old saw about the genie and the bottle is true...Your successful efforts to secure information regarding Elke is worthy of Gold Stars! The name of Elke Guttenbach has been my most closely guarded secret for the last thirty-five years. I owe her both an explanation and an apology, but I have no idea what the reaction might be if contact were made."

A day later, he wrote Ingrid, "After reading, re-reading, and re-rereading your e-mail, I'm left with the unmistakable impression you are convinced that my contacting Elke would be at least acceptable if not welcome. I make no pretense about understanding women's intuition and would certainly not attempt to disparage it, but I sure hope you are correct." Ingrid replied that she had no sixth sense, just a Platonic desire to reconnect old friends and lovers. What people call intuition, she suspected, was just "reason in desperate straits and lots of free time."

Early August came and Gary wrote, "I have finally admitted to myself exactly what happened with Elke. Losing at anything is anathema to me. It's a form of banishment or excommunication. When in my juvenile wisdom thirty-seven years ago I toted up the pluses and minuses, and the odds of success didn't look good, I left her rather than lose her even though I'd sworn to write...It's such a terrible thing to admit—an absolute betrayal."

By mid-August, Gary was feverishly restocking his horse barn to keep his mind off a woman who didn't know he was still alive, but when he was through "stacking hundreds of hay bales," he asked Ingrid if she would "fly to Berlin with my e-mails in hand." We both thought he was joking until we received the following: "Ingrid, I've decided to send Elke a dozen roses and a laptop."

When I asked if he were serious, he replied cryptically, "A tiger has me by the tail, and I'm digging myself a hole..." I wanted to say, "Then stop digging!" because I thought he was certifiable at this point, but Ingrid, who was fueling his fantasies, held out hope that Elke might eventually write, "Fly to Berlin posthaste, my love!"

Then Gary casually mentioned that he was married and had been for the last thirty-six years. Sixty e-mails were stacked in my computer, not one of which mentioned a wife or his two children.

Over the next few days it became apparent that Martha, Gary's wife, had discovered the e-mails mentioning Elke, roses, laptops, a passport, etc. and angrily demanded an explanation. We would have appreciated one too. Did he fear that mentioning his wife would curb our efforts to find Elke and renew their intercontinental courtship? A snail-mail posting said, "I must beg your indulgence for at least a while. This 'sorting out' could take a very long time. I cannot assume my e-mails are private... The marriage that I thought was doused years ago has some fire left. A thirty-six-year investment bears some consideration, and I don't want to exacerbate the situation. Don't know how it's going to turn out or what I'll do about Elke."

Using an email address Martha knew nothing of, Ingrid talked him out of sending the roses and the laptop by telling him that, if she were in Elke's shoes, such a gift would come with "needy" or "desperate" written all over it. So Gary simply wrote the following:

Dear Elke,

Thirty-eight years ago today, you sent me a postcard from Berlin. I have enclosed a copy of that postcard. Since I have no idea if you remember who I am, I've also enclosed a photo of myself from 1962. A lifetime of events has transpired for both of us during the last thirty-eight years. If you elect not to respond, I will understand, and you will remain as you have been all these years, a beautiful golden memory.

Gary

The day before Gary received Elke's reply, he wondered if, ironically, she might be the catalyst to put his marriage back together rather than destroy it. "If so," he added, "I'll chalk it up to one more instance of celestial humor." Twelve days after Gary wrote the above, he received Elke's reply, coolly inquiring, "How did you locate me?" It was not exactly the response he was hoping for, but she did include some photographs and an e-mail address.

With these tokens in hand, Martha was sure that Gary "had opened Pandora's box" because, among other things, Elke revealed that she had written Gary many letters to his parents' address, the only one he had when he left Germany in 1962. She reminded him of their "holy oath" to write. Why, if he had feelings for her, she wanted to know, had he not written back? How Elke's postcard reached him and why he didn't answer with more than a card and a question about the VW engine he'd left behind was something he could not explain. Gary surmised that his parents, now dead, destroyed the letters because they did not want their son marrying a German.

By the middle of October, Martha was growing more comfortable with Gary and Elke's correspondence following some liberal doses of counseling. Furthermore, both of them realized that Elke was happily wed and that Gary loved his horses too much to leave the States. Martha's health was another question. When she had her gall bladder removed, Gary was the soul of selflessness.

January came and Gary took a part-time job in a book store to learn the book trade and a job in a coffee shop to learn how to make lattes and pastries. Ingrid and I helped to convince him that the "spy-book reader" was too narrow a market, so he decided to cater to the "feminine book trade" perhaps hoping that Elke would enter one day in a flapper costume.

The snows fell heavily on Michigan in January of 2001, and in one e-mail Gary said he suspected that Martha followed him out to the barn after each heavy snow to mark the location of his frozen body. Ingrid and I thought the remark was morbid, but perhaps it was a premonition. By the end of the month, he was complaining of retinal bleeding, high blood pressure, kidney stones, a failed EKG, and generally "feeling like shit."

In May, Elke wrote us inquiring about Gary; he was "MIA," and she was worried. He'd told her in February that he'd gone to a doctor "to have a flat fixed" and was told that he "needed a new engine." He said he was worried about a "dark spot on the CAT scan that no one could explain." Though I blithely assured her there was little cause to worry, Gary was dead by June.

ೞ

According to the postmaster in Verona, about a thousand letters are sent to Juliet Capulet each year, many of which are written by men like Gary with an itch they cannot scratch. They jokingly complain, as Gary once did, that "men chase women until the women catch their men," but intimacy is difficult for many whether they are the chased or the chasee. Having allowed a lover to slip away, they lose their love of the hunt and settle for something from the grocer. Then they complain of thirst standing knee-deep in fresh-running water with a tuna sandwich in their creel. Gary was certain that Elke was the answer to the questions etched in his heart. He had hoped to sweep her off her feet with roses and some high-tech gifts, but her feet were nailed to the floor. Ironically, the answer to his question was sitting across the breakfast table.

HEARTBREAK HOTEL REVISITED: LONELINESS

"The cure for loneliness is solitude."
—Marianne Moore

"Solitude is to the mind what fasting is to the body…
—Marquis de Vauvenargues

"Lonesome George," the last living Pinta Island Giant Tortoise, wanders his Galapagos sanctuary like the last Japanese soldier on Guam twenty-eight years after his superiors had surrendered. A vegetarian victim of a black-rat infestation, George apparently has not given up hope of finding a mate though all Pinta-Island-Giant-Tortoise DNA except for his own has been consumed by the rats. George eagerly lifts his hundred-year-old head to greet his keeper, but all the human can give him is the chlorophyll and fiber which sustain him. His exquisite alienation is akin to Einstein's when a dozen people in the world understood what he was doing, and the Nazis were burning his books. He's Squanto, the sole survivor of a smallpox epidemic that killed his tribe, or the last speaker of Eyak inhabiting a corner of Alaska where even God speaks English. It was a lonely human who first populated the void with gods, much the way I turn on the radio in an empty house.

The closest I have come to the existential solitude of George were the days following my departure from my family when I went off to Georgia Tech at age seventeen. I slumped on the bottom bunk exhausted, mourning my loss. That lasted until my roommate Homer Harrison appeared a day later with the worst case of acne I'd ever seen. I couldn't have cared less; he had an intelligent voice. Loneliness, however, returned the following semester after dropping out of Tech. Riding the bus to Ft. Jackson for my basic army training with forty strangers, I yearned to belong to someone somewhere. That was fifty years ago, and I have no desire to revisit the time I was allergic to the world.

If you've ever been a "bubble boy" even for a short while, it may come as a surprise that isolation is often targeted by cartoonists. Edward Koren pictures two campers sitting beside a campfire as one picks up his cell phone and says, "Who can we call?" In similar fashion, Robert Weber draws two monks walking the cloisters under a dim moon. Says one monk, "I always feel a tad secular on Saturday night." And Bruce Eric Kaplan's balding, overweight anti-hero, alone in his tidy den, answers the phone and says, "I'd love to, but I have a million lonely ritualistic things I need to do." I suppose the point is with the Earth's population currently at an all-time high, a human's chances of finding a mate have never been better.

If you're a firefly who cannot find someone broadcasting a compatible signal, Robert Frost argues that "boughten friendship" will suffice. When a dean I had worked for retired, he proactively found five fellows in the college who enjoyed playing poker, and told us the drinks and snacks were on him. To join the party, he said, "Just show up every Wednesday at eight and be ready to play until eleven." It was one of the most convivial groups I have ever been part of, and every one of us knew we'd been purchased to provide our old boss a social life. The free beer had a lot to do with it but so did the chance to get out of the house and talk to some friends.

Americans who find they're bowling alone or playing a lot of solitaire have found their percentage of the population growing from near zero in 1900 to 25% in 2011. Many restaurants now offer single diners "maverick tables" for those faced with the unhappy prospect of eating alone. I keep hearing of people buying a floor buffer "to have something to do" or calling an 800-number "to have someone to talk to." Some of the emptiest halls I've frequented angle endlessly through the warehouses for the elderly. In Germany, there's a CD on the market titled *Alone No More,* which plays the simulated sounds another person might make rattling around in a house like a bat in the attic. Aimed at people who have everything but someone to share it with, the recording promises "sixty-two minutes of togetherness" to help the listener "feel cared for but not disturbed." Personally, I'd rather slip a Vivaldi CD in the player or turn on NPR.

Unlike the cartoonists above, most visual artists have a more sober assessment of the lonely, which often includes themselves. Crowd scenes and couples lack the traction in our memory that the solitary figure obtains. Whether it's a painter working on a landscape, a solitary woman in an all-night diner, or a solo hiker in the moonlight, neither the convivial group nor the angry mob burrows quite as deeply into the cockles of our hearts. Edward Hopper, Andrew Wyeth, Caspar David Friedrich among others made considerable fortunes from the estranged romantic torments of those who chose "the road less travelled." As much as I admire it, a reproduction of Rembrandt's *Night Watch* will never replace my framed copy of Dürer's *St. Jerome in His Study,* for solitude is my creative well.

Country music offers another fine kettle of fish and chips, mixing the serious with the comic. Juxtapose, for example, "Oh, Lonesome Me" with "I'm So Lonesome I Could Go Out and Ride Around on I-285." The Caucasian blues have a unique way of consoling a solitary fellow slumped at the bar before spilling a beer down his pants. Indeed, there are those who just need to "man up and get over it."

Be that as it may, consider a neighbor of ours: he or she drives up to a brick house most evenings, opens the garage door from behind tinted windows, enters the garage, and shuts the door. No one I know has ever seen this person, who hires someone to mow the lawn and doesn't have a newspaper delivered. There are no children, pets, or trees to fill up the gutters, and come Halloween, the lights are off. Yet in this fortress of solitude may live a very productive soul who perhaps has learned that life is better lived alone than in bad company. Like Jeffrey Dahmer who cut up and froze his victims to prevent their departure, I fear I would wither and wane living like the person down the street. Assuming my arms are long enough, I'm one of the people playing cards with my neighbors in solitary confinement.

But then there's Greta Garbo, the beautiful Swedish actress who never married or had children, and who is best remembered for a line from *Grand Hotel* (1932): "I want to be alone." Perhaps because she uttered variations of this line in other films, her fans took it as a personal manifesto when she left Hollywood at thirty-six and moved into a New York apartment. When asked by a reporter, Garbo replied, "I never said, 'I want to be alone [in reference to myself].' I only said, 'I want to be *left* alone.'" Wealthy, content, and possibly lesbian, Garbo refused to overstay her welcome in the public eye. Though it's not for me, I have to respect a decision to leave the bright lights and spin a cocoon from the silk of a self.

Owning Up to the Avalanche: Responsibility

"The buck doesn't even slow down here."
—Anonymous

"Shoulder your small part with a fragrant grace—
every rose petal holds the moon in place."
—The Wordspinner

In 2011, a woman in El Paso County found my ninety-four-year-old father with a fractured kneecap and shattered wrist on a remote section of her ranch. It's a long story that I won't tell here, but she called 911 on her cell phone as soon as she realized the rapidly deteriorating condition Dad was in. Then she provided shade and comfort but no water as directed until the ambulance arrived. The call was crucial according to the EMS personnel: another hour in the triple-digit temperatures probably would have killed him. Indeed, the Samaritan's initial reaction was to turn away, suspecting that my father's red Cadillac belonged to a drug dealer, but something drew her along the unpaved road before realizing that Dad was desperate. Though she had responsibilities of her own, she stayed by his side until help arrived.

Responsibility has a way of taking some people by surprise, and apparently, I'm one of them. Sometimes, I remind myself of the fundamentalist farmer who turned away three rescue vehicles in a flood. Standing at the pearly gates, he grumbles, "Why didn't you rapture me off the rooftop; I kept the faith." God replies, "Don't blame me; I sent two boats and a helicopter."

When the triplets who live across the street asked me to take them on a bike ride, I thought I was doing my neighborly duty by them. I'd seen them at their school earlier in the day where they told me it was their seventh birthday. "Mr. Skip, can we go for a bike ride," they begged like starved nestlings to the puzzlement of their teacher who was herding her first graders back into the classroom. I agreed to take them; it was their birthday after all, and they promised me cake.

After a spin class that evening, I drove home and saw two of them riding their bikes in front of their house on our dead-end street. Recalling the promise I'd made at school, I drove into the garage and went to get my bike. Michael, a fraternal triplet, rode up as I was putting on my helmet and said, "Mommy said we can go with you, but it has to be a short one." A short one was fine with me because these three on bicycles are a trial, and it was getting late. Once when we were riding on their school's campus, I saw a car approaching and yelled, "Move to the right!" One went left and stopped; one tumbled into the grassy median, and the other sped past me on the right. Fortunately, there was very little traffic that Sunday, and what there was was moving slowly. After the ride, I asked them to raise their right hands, and two raised their left. That had been a few months earlier; in the interim, I hoped they'd learned to distinguish one hand from another.

The triplets' mother was inside, and the ride I had in mind was two miles or less, so I gathered my fledglings and said, "Now look, boy and girls, I'm the boss, so listen to me when I tell you to do something." I asked them to knock on their helmets with their left hand, which they did. I was reassured, but I shouldn't have been.

Off we went down Blue Ridge Drive, weaving and wobbling like drunken bees. Our initial destination was "Wolf Street," a name we'd given Karen Circle where an arthritic German shepherd barks at squirrels and kids on bikes. The "wolf" was indoors, so we made a right onto Karen Drive as I yelled, "Get on the sidewalk!" Michael as usual was twenty yards ahead of his sisters, so I shouted, "Stop at the next stop sign and wait for Maryanne!" She usually rides twenty yards behind to avoid being sideswiped by her brother. When I reached the intersection of Karen and Berkley Drive, Michael and Margaret were straddling their bikes looking at the sunset. As I joined them, I looked over my shoulder and saw their sister coming down the hill on the right side of the street. I began looking and listening for any approaching cars at this blind intersection, and as I glanced to my right, Maryanne crossed four lanes of Berkley without a trace of indecision. Thank heaven no cars were coming, but I yelled for her to wait for us on the other side of the road. When we reached her, I was trembling. "I told you to stop—didn't you hear me? Listen, Sweetie, dry your tears on your sleeve, but you must know that crossing this street as you did is very dangerous—you might have been killed. Drivers cannot see you on this curve."

I reviewed the rules of the road for the kids and reminded myself that while self-interest precludes perfect charity, the essence of wrong *is* self-interest. Back home, I told their mother what had happened, but she was expecting a Skype call from her ex. Perhaps not comprehending the gravity of the situation, she just said, "Okay, I'll speak to her."

As Stanislaw Lec observed, "No snowflake in the avalanche ever feels responsible." Though I'd been a solitary flake, as the largest and oldest, I did feel responsible. Had a car or truck been rounding that bend, two and perhaps three of us would have died. That night I dreamed I placed my young wife on the handlebars of an old Schwinn with a radio fuselage and went for a ride in a bad neighborhood. Someone on the radio was singing "Daisy Bell...I'm half-crazy...on a bicycle built for two." Then my front wheel dropped into an open manhole pitching my bride headlong under a passing car. In a noirish courtroom, I sued the city for their carelessness and Schwinn for their failure to warn me about sitting on the handlebars. I awoke in a sweat.

Had there been an accident, of course, I would have been financially, morally, and perhaps criminally responsible, and this realization still congeals the contents of my stomach. I never should have taken those kids across that thoroughfare without their mother's explicit permission even if the kids did look like orphans and it was their birthday. Hindus say, "Call on the Gods, but row away from the rocks." There were alternatives "away from the rocks" that I never considered, and I should have. The airlines say that when oxygen masks fall from the ceiling, you should attend to yourself first. This experience with Maryanne has convinced me otherwise.

A Family of Scofflaws: Disobedience

"Hitler is always right."
—Rudolf Hess

"Human history began with an act of disobedience—it is likely to end with an act of obedience."
—Erich Fromm

Shortly after World War II ended, the American eugenist, General Frederick Osborn paid Gertrude Stein a visit in France. What, he wondered, could the Allies do to educate the Germans so that another war would not be fought over the same blood-soaked territory? Stein answered, "Teach them disobedience. [Teach them not to] believe everything their fathers or teachers tell them."

I was four when Stein issued that radical prescription, and except for the time I ran away from home, I don't think I ever seriously considered disobedience before my testicles began pumping testosterone. For thirteen years, I was closer to Sid Sawyer than Tom, and my "running away" on a fenced-in military base was more a getting lost than a violation of my parents' rules. However, the German family I would eventually become part of was well into its first over-the-counter bottle of Stein's noncompliance pills before the war ended.

Aunt Elfriede, a baker's wife who lived at the foot of the Hartz Mountains, was the first of these scofflaws. Before the war, she and her husband ran a small bakery in the village of Vienenburg. During the conflict, they did their best to continue running the business despite the heavy loss of clientele. In 1943, Uncle Albert was called to serve in the *Wehrmacht* despite the fact that he was sixty and in declining health. Elfriede, however, decided to continue the shop's operations, so she could qualify for the flour allotment her neighbors depended on. One day she received a letter from Ilse Barmwater, a niece living in Wolsdorf, a village about fifty miles to the north. The letter from my future mother-in-law told of her desperate attempts to feed herself and her two children after her husband had left for the Eastern Front in 1939. Elfriede knew it was impossible for her to travel to Wolsdorf or send something as large as a loaf of bread by parcel post, so when her customers made a purchase, she struck their ration stamps with her knuckle as she palmed the rubber stamp. At the end of the day, she taped a few of the uncanceled stamps to a piece of paper, folded it in two, placed it in an envelope, and sent it to Ilse. Every few weeks, she risked her family's livelihood in order that her niece's family had enough to eat.

Meanwhile, Ilse was not just writing letters. She worked for every village farmer who would hire her to plant, weed, and bring in a harvest. For her labors, she was paid with a small share of the bounty. She shook milk in the dead of night to make contraband butter, bartered for food with garments sewn from a parachute her husband had sent home, and slaughtered an illegally purchased sheep to make mutton sausage. She also stole sugar beets from one of the local farms when the owner told her, "The law won't let me sell you any beets, Ilse, but I cannot stop you from stealing some."

My favorite story of Ilse's disobedience occurred just a few weeks before the European war ended in May of 1945. The BBC, which Ilse's father had defiantly listened to through most of the war, predicted that British infantry would soon be arriving on their way to Berlin. As allied bombers flew overhead without being challenged by the *Luftwaffe*, the enemy's version of events seemed closer to the truth than German radio reported. As the rumors mounted, the staunch Nazi mayor of Wolsdorf rose to the challenge and ordered every able-bodied person to fill sandbags and stack them at the narrow intersection near the Schulenburg Tavern on the road leading east. As the women filled canvas bags, the talk naturally turned to sabotage when they realized that a sandbag barricade was not going to stop a tank, and their homes might be shelled by an irritated foe. They agreed, therefore, to return late one night. Armed with kitchen knives, a dozen women slit the bags turning the barricade into little more than a speed bump. The mayor was furious, but what could he do—he had no suspects, and the tanks were already in Warberg, the next village to the west. When the tanks came, they barely slowed down.

Two and a half years after peace had been declared, my father-in-law returned home from the south of France, where he'd been held as a POW. It didn't take him long to see that the deprivations his family were suffering were worse than they had endured during the war. Being unemployed, he couldn't do much about their finances, but he could relieve the firewood shortage. With his young son and daughter beside him, he pulled a wagon he'd built into the Eitz, a state-owned forest about a mile away from Wolsdorf. The law, which dated to the seventeenth century, forbade the gathering of any wood except what disease or the weather had caused to fall. Unfortunately for Otto, the forest was picked clean, and there was this finical forester who made random inspection trips. But as the Germans say, there's more than one way to pluck a goose. With Ingrid stationed a hundred meters to the north and Rolf to the south, Otto felt safe pulling down dead branches with a rope tied to a brass weight. The law requiring the branches to fall naturally made no sense: most of that wood was so porous it was worthless for heating or cooking. The family needed the fuel now, and he took it. What he and the children could not pile onto the wagon for the nocturnal trip home, they hid beneath leaves until they could safely return.

My wife learned her lessons in principled disobedience from the silent hands of her family. When the law or the lawgiver was clearly wrong, she felt no compunction violating the rules though she never stepped so far over the line as her parents had because it wasn't necessary. When Ingrid was fifteen, she was one of the top sprinters in the county. At track practice late one day, the ex-Nazi track coach insisted that the sprinters kneel on the cinder track even though some of the girls' knees were bleeding. Ingrid quietly gathered herself a wad of grass from the infield and placed the cushion under her right knee. When the coach discovered this violation, she struck her star sprinter across the shoulders with the drum stick she carried to beat the tambourine in rhythmic gymnastics. When she threatened to strike again, Ingrid dashed out from under her and shinnied up the sportground flag pole. Her perch was hardly comfortable, but she stayed there until the bell rang a short while later and the coach left. To a former Nazi, the peremptory clang of a school bell had the force of law. To Ingrid, it just meant practice was over.

After World War II, the reformed German government abolished the judge advocate's division, which meant that if a *Bundeswehr* soldier goes AWOL, he or she is tried in a civil court. Furthermore, German soldiers are expressly required to defy orders that one of ordinary intelligence should know violates the criminal code. Gertrude Stein's advice, it seems, had been taken to heart.

TALKING BACK TO THE RECORDED MESSAGE: AUTHORITY

"The gods I worshipped demanded the dance of death. I had no other choice..."
—Adolf Eichmann

"Galileo's raised middle finger points at the Vatican."
—The Wordspinner

Perhaps because I grew up under the heavy hand of a military father, I had a hard time disciplining my own children, for I often found it easier to do their chores than raise my voice. Dad struck me a few times, but he usually didn't need force: his Gorgonian stare could turn the contents of my stomach to stone. I'm sure that look of menacing authority served him well leading 660 combat engineers across Germany in 1945, for he did not lose a single man in the conflict that claimed fifty-five million lives. But if fear is the primary emotion associated with a parent, what does that portend for the commonwealth? In my case, it has meant that my father and I are civil, but we don't fish, travel, or golf together either,—never have.

Underused power, on the other hand, is as bad as that which is overused. I recall reading a newspaper account of a mother and her sickly daughter riding a Chicago city bus. Though the girl was wearing a pacemaker, it did not prevent her from having a massive heart attack. Knowing the downtown area well, the mother begged the driver to take them to a hospital, which was only a block away. The shaken driver said he was sorry, but the rules did not allow any deviation from his route. At the next scheduled stop, he let his frantic passenger and her daughter off. A man who'd been waiting for the bus quickly appraised the situation and volunteered to carry the ninety-pound, unconscious girl to the hospital. He made it, but it was too late to save her. In the movies, the Samaritan would have commandeered the bus and saved the girl's life, but reality often wears a different face. The frightened bus driver was so policy-bound he could not see the forest for the rules.

In Philip Roth's short story, "The Conversion of the Jews," Rabbi Binder is also bound by policy, but he uses his authority very differently. When Ozzie, a *bar mitzvah* student, challenges three thousand years of Jewish belief, Binder strikes him. Bleeding from his nose, Ozzie races to the roof and threatens to jump unless his teacher and his screaming classmates below agree to consider that the ancient beliefs *might* be wrong. I'll never forget a sophomore saying in a discussion of the story, "I'd let my kid jump before

I swore allegiance to anyone but Jesus." This twenty-year-old, who missed Roth's ecumenical point, had all the earmarks of the policy-bound adult that she was on the brink of becoming.

Rather than have a dead child on his hands, Roth's rabbi "converted" to Christianity, but forced conversions are the wooden nickels of faith. Nevertheless, children do possess a moral authority disproportionate to their intellectual and physical development. Recently, a neighbor opened her door to a peddler of some "miracle cleaner." You should know that this woman is raising three small children almost single-handedly while her husband is serving overseas as a translator for a private contractor. Over the last five years, he's been home about five months. When the doorbell rang, all the children ran outside to see who was there. The peddler, nervous in the sudden mob, pushed Michael, the six-year-old "man of the family," away, and in doing so, accidentally marked his t-shirt with some green ink he'd intended to use in a demonstration of his "miracle." While the mother went to the telephone, Michael said, "I think you should leave now," and the peddler did.

Later, the mother said she felt sorry for the salesman as he slouched off to the house next door, for the mercantile spirit had left him. Only the sadist enjoys humiliation whether it's deserved or not. My uncle liked to tell of the time he watched my father, a full-bird colonel, being "chewed out" by a staff sergeant. Uncle Bob was an eighteen-year-old airman stationed at Ft. Benning while my forty-year-old father was there trying to win his "jump wings." One day, Bob took some time off from his round of deliveries to see if he could spot his brother-in-law in the new class of trainees jumping from various platforms into the sawdust pit. As luck would have it, Bob witnessed Dad violating the rule of looking down before landing. That's when the fire-plug of a jumpmaster attacked Dad in spray of saliva. Bob thought the scene was hilarious, but I've always felt sorry for my old man.

In too many instances especially after he retired, Dad was humbled by my mother. On one occasion she had bought a clematis vine and wanted it planted next to the mailbox to beautify the support. For Dad, who was in his eighties, this meant a long, uphill hike to fetch a shovel, so he was arguing for another location near the back porch, "where we can see and enjoy it." They went back and forth several times, until Mother, pointing at the mailbox, said, "Butch, dig a hole!" Dad knew he was licked, and as he walked to the garden shed, he looked like a veteran soccer player being sent off with a red card in front of his fans.

But honestly, I cannot figure myself out sometimes. One minute I'm against all authority, and the next, I'm feeling sorry for the cock of the walk that's been bumped from the roost. My old boss, Dean Morris Cox handled disrespect as well as anyone I've ever seen. When the summer softball league opened, he was invited to play with a group of his faculty. Trouble was, he'd never played softball, but he had donated $100 for bats and balls. On opening day, he arrived wearing Bermuda shorts, black nylon socks, and golf spikes. Unceremoniously, an eighteen-year-old umpire ejected him from the game before he hurt someone. Quietly, Morris left but returned a few minutes later in tennis shoes, and the manager immediately put him in the lineup. The freshman umpire wasn't General MacArthur telling the Emperor of Japan he was no longer a god, but it was close. Both the dean and the emperor handled public humiliation with more aplomb than I could muster.

Some libertarians have argued that each of us regardless of our authority deserves a personal veto. I would not go to that extreme because I've long admired the moderate position Supreme Court Justice Abe Fortas staked out: "I am a man of the law...But had I lived in Germany in Hitler's days, I hope I would have refused to wear an armband, to *Heil Hitler,* [and] to submit to genocide. This I hope, although Hitler's edicts were law..."

In a nutshell, I'd break ranks and dodge the cannonball I saw coming my way while harboring the greatest respect for those who stood there and took it. Lucky for me, I wasn't at Waterloo.

Visible Emotion: Tears

"Tears helped Nixon and hurt Muskie."
—The Wordspinner

"Men who never get carried away should be."
—Malcolm Forbes

When my wife, Ingrid, was about fifteen and some alien spirit moved her, she would go upstairs, close her bedroom door, turn the radio on, and search for a sad song. Sitting before her vanity mirror imagining some fedora-topped lover to whom she was saying *Auf Wiedersehen*, she'd sing into her "microphone" until her eyes were wet with pleasure. Other women, I've heard, cry every time they take Holy Communion.

I have to confess that a self- or Jesus-induced "good cry" may be the only emotional release I've never utilized. For years, my tears came infrequently in part because my parents discouraged them. I cannot recall seeing either one of them cry until we started visiting my South Georgia grandparents when I was about thirteen. Those summer visits were so enjoyable that when we left, Mother, my two sisters, and I would weep but never whimper or snivel from Columbus halfway to the outskirts of Atlanta in a quiet fit of self-pity.

Meanwhile, Dad never shed a tear; he just drove and kept whatever disappointment he felt in his lachrymose family to himself. He comes from the stoic Midwestern and military traditions perhaps best epitomized by the Norwegian-Minnesotan widower who said, "I loved my wife so, I almost told her once." At the other end of this spectrum is the contemporary essayist Roger Rosenblatt who wrote his daughter before her wedding, "Don't mind me when I cry. It's just my way of enjoying myself." For years I thought I fell somewhere between the emotionally stunted and the wellsprings of exuberance, for often my eyes would swim but not slop over onto the deck. That is assuming the surface tension was correct and I kept my eyelids beating fast enough to evaporate the excess. Though I wept when my closest friend, my father-in-law, and my mother died, I was not "red-eyed in sackcloth" when the Braves or John Kerry lost.

When Ingrid's father died in Germany, our family happened to be vacationing at Cherry Grove, a beach community in South Carolina that my in-laws loved better than home itself. The phone call, which we'd feared for weeks, came at 6 in the morning. We all sat on the bed, held each other, and cried. All except our son, Shane, who at the time was a twenty-three-year-old graduate student in drama. Though I said nothing, I worried about his unnatural restraint until a year later when his close friend Earl died in a plane crash. At the funeral for this young Marine pilot whose body was never recovered from the Pacific, I watched with relief as Shane's eyes suffused with tears, satisfied that he'd surmounted the final cusp of emotional maturity.

In medieval Europe, many in the medical profession felt that the effect of crying was like any purgative acting on the stomach or the bowels. Like a good blow of the nose, tears were beneficial because they emptied the saturated brain, which in turn aided reason. In eighteenth-century England, there were those who equated masculine tears with moral worth, not to mention sensitivity. And today, some Muslims feel that weeping is a sign of spiritual maturity because reading poignant passages in the Qur'an demands tears of the true believer.

As I said, when it came to tears, I'd always considered myself somewhere in the middle. That is until Ingrid and I went to see a Met simulcast of *Madama Butterfly* in Greenville recently. Now I had wept over operas before; indeed, once after showing the last act of *La Bohème* to a class of college juniors, I was still in mourning for Mimi when the student nearest the switch turned on the lights. As I reached for my handkerchief, I quickly reminded my uncomfortable class that opera fails when the audience departs with dry eyes, but I don't think they were convinced because they scurried away without a consoling word for their grieving instructor.

The Anthony Mingella production of *Butterfly*, however, is an affective triumph, for I and most of the people around me wept at Butterfly's wedding in Act I, her suicide in Act III, and several scenes in between. By the conclusion, my heart was so full, I thought it would burst for this innocent victim of American colonialism. When Butterfly sliced her carotid artery, and two figures in black pulled thirty feet of billowing red silk from her kimono, I gasped audibly and clutched my neck to stanch the loss. This was one time I was grateful that no one could reach the light switch.

Mingella's rice paper spare but deceptively rich production reminded me that strumming our interior harps is foremost what art is about. Irony and sarcasm have their places, but as E. E. Cummings wrote, "feeling is first." Many post modernists seem to have forgotten the lesson taught perhaps best by Harriet Beecher Stowe when she brought much of the nation to its knees by separating several sympathetic slaves from their families. After winning the hearts of the North, war was inevitable.

The South cried foul, but they knew Achilles had wept for the loss of his friend and Jesus for the excruciating pain of the cross. Some might condemn these displays as mawkish, but brief as they are, I cannot. Scarlett would weep again for Tara in the 1930s, but today most Confederate ducts are dry. Nevertheless, many Southern women still spend their afternoons filling an emotional void watching one more episode of "sunlight on the soapsuds." That said, I'll never forget coming home early once, and finding our neighbor and landlady sitting on the floor of our duplex, weeping over *As the World Turns*. I wasn't about to begrudge this poor woman her mite, and I told her to use our television any time hers was in the shop. A friend said our neighbor was "just going through the emotions," but if she felt better, who was I to criticize.

Now Hitler is another case. He reportedly cried when his dog Blondi died, yet he never shed a tear for the millions killed in that insane experiment to stimulate the German economy. But then Napoleon had warned the world a century earlier that "the heart of a statesman should be in his head." In most cases, this is good advice—a Warren Christopher or Hillary Clinton bawling at the Wailing Wall when the Israelis announce they are not going to vacate the West Bank surely is not a smart diplomatic expression in the machismo atmosphere of the Middle East. One reason women live longer, so the theory goes, is that they flush their systems more frequently than men do. As for me, I can't wait until Mingella's *Butterfly* is available on DVD.

ALLIGATOR IN A SHOE FACTORY: FEAR

"Take no counsel from your fears."
—Stonewall Jackson

"Take the counsel of your fears."
—American proverb

My father still tells the story that he heard from an Army Air Corps friend in 1944. It seems that a B-17 was struck by antiaircraft fire returning from a bombing run over Germany. The plane's engines were untouched, but part of the electrical and all of the hydraulic systems were disabled. The situation called for a belly landing after dumping excess fuel because the landing gear was immobilized. As the bomb and gun crew gathered behind a bulkhead, the crew chief noted that his ventral gunner was missing. Upon inspection, the chief realized that the hatch to the cramped pod could not be manually opened. When he finally found the words recoiling in his larynx, the chief informed the gunner what was about to transpire—a landing that would crush the bottom of the aircraft in order to spare the rest. The young man's last words were unintelligible over the roar of the engines, but if God was anywhere near "this other Eden," He surely heard the gunner's screams.

I suppose I was about ten when I heard my father carelessly tell that story. Sixty years later, I still have nightmares of the runway rising to meet twenty tons of metal. In between the bomber and the concrete was an acutely conscious airman witnessing his final landing from a vantage better than the pilot's but worse than divine providence.

Fundamentalist preachers love black-and-white questions like: "Will you be ready when the black plane of death circles overhead?" In 2008, at an anti-gay marriage rally in California, an evangelist asked, "What's more important—respect for others or the fear of God?" Of course, only a saint is going to think of others when the bullet with her name on it gets close enough to read. I'm not sure whether I will fear God at that point or fear the bullet, but I'm reasonably sure I won't be thinking of anyone beside myself. Call me self-absorbed if you like, but no one dies without some personal regrets.

The choice of respecting others or fearing God is complex if one reads the Old Testament and the literature based on it with an open mind. I recall reading *Samson Agonistes* as an undergraduate and thinking Milton neglected to tell Samuel's story of three hundred foxes set on fire to burn the Philistine's crops because the British moralist surely disapproved of the animal's torture. Professor Miller assured me that Milton *did* approve of the fiery deaths the same way he supported the indiscriminate killing of Philistines. Thousands died, and surely, I argued, some of them were innocent. The professor red-penciled my essay with a yawning *C*, and I've been afraid of Milton ever since.

I lost my fear of God, however, a long time ago, but I still pay Him and His creation a nodding respect. I've looked down the barrel of an East German border guard's AK-47, gone weak in the knees hanging drapes in a ninth-story office, shivered uncontrollably in surgery, and waited for a surgeon to tell me that my wife was going to be okay, so I think I know the emotion I am speaking of. It is not what one feels finger-filtering a horror film or jumping a diamondback rattler on a downhill run in Arizona. Though laughter often allays stress, it does not as a rule accompany the real threat of serious bodily injury.

As a longtime member of a municipal recreation center's board of advisors, I take a proprietary interest in the facility where I exercise a few times a week. This has never been truer than when budget cuts forced the center's director to eliminate the weight-room supervisors, whose job was to maintain the sign-in sheet and keep kids under twelve safely outside. One blue-shirted employee's simple presence also added an important element that I've recently come to appreciate: civility.

One afternoon, I was using the quadriceps machine while ten feet away another patron was using the leg-squat machine. For reasons known only to him, this well-built young man grunted conspicuously with each repetition, and when he finished a set, he dropped four hundred pounds several inches on to the weight stand. It was steel on steel making a noise well in excess of 100 decibels. Finally, I had all I could take, and I said in the least challenging voice I could muster, "You know, if you break that machine, no one will be able to use it, including you."

Leaping to his feet, the heavyweight lifter said, "Mind your own business, old man! I've paid my dues. You stupid!"

I denied myself a stress-reducing laugh and said, "Excuse me, but what does that sign behind you say? I can't read it from here."

"It says, 'Please don't drop the weights.'"

"Well?" I said as my mouth went dry.

"I didn't drop the weights," he said, slipping two forty-five-pound disks from his bar. "*This* is dropping weights," he said, tossing one disk about ten feet to his left and another to his right.

"No," I said rising from my own machine, "That's not dropping, that's throwing." With my heart hammering in my ears, I went to get my jacket and left by the back door. A half dozen or more people were in the room when the flash point was reached, but no one spoke a word. Quite simply, we were struck dumb with terror. In less than a minute, we'd all become that small Jewish boy, hands overhead, being herded down the street by several Nazi thugs. Fear has a way of multiplying and magnifying the foe.

As a board member, I knew the exercise room has four cameras that record almost everything that goes on, but, of course, it never occurred to me to tell the weight hurler that everything he'd done had been captured on a CD. That would have given *him* something to think about. As for me, I suffered two nights of insomnia and found several reasons to change my weight-lifting routine.

Fear, however, is not always so palpable. Some friends of ours recently built their dream retirement home including a bedroom for their daughter-in-law, who lives two thousand miles distant. The young woman is germ- and pyrophobic, so her East Coast bedroom features a toilet separated from the shower and sink by four walls and a door. It also has a ground-level exit in case the all-brick house burns on the one weekend a year she's expected to reside there. It all has to do with compartmentalizing one's apprehensions, our friends assure us. I wish it were that easy; I can corral my own fears while the sun is up, but they keep jumping the fence at night.

Judging from some crime statistics, Americans have never been safer, yet the international prophets of doom say that the Death of Nature is just over the horizon given the untold fingers on untold nuclear devices. As a consequence, I fear I'm a version of that old *Frank and Ernest* cartoon in which Frank hears Dr. Ernest declare, "You're phobophobic." To which Frank says, "I was afraid of that."

STARDUST SPRINKLERS AND SOBS: GRANDPARENTS

"Over the river and through the woods, to grandfather's house we go."
—Lydia Maria Child

"Grandparents who want to be truly helpful will do well to keep their mouths shut and their opinions to themselves until these are requested."
—Dr. T. Berry Brazelton

An old story begins with the observation that grandchildren and grandparents are "natural allies" with a "common enemy." I've never felt quite so common as when our son was sixteen and struggling with girls, grades, sports, and me. That summer, my German in-laws came for a month long visit, and by some stroke of good fortune, my father-in-law thought to bring his harmonica though he had no advance notice that his grandson was trying to teach himself the blues harp. When these two discovered their common interest, I backed off. In the cool of the evening over the next few weeks, I would pull up a chair on the patio's perimeter and listen to their jamming. I recall thinking that the harmonizing, which left me feeling marginalized, was a bit like the monkey bars at school recess: one can make smoother progress if one skips a bar. Indeed, parents often *are* the bar that some adolescents would do well to bypass.

I rarely had this luxury myself because our peripatetic family seldom lived very close to my mother's parents and never near my father's. But I won't forget the times that "Dear," my maternal grandmother, bought me an ice cream and showed me off at Kirven's, her favorite department store. Every child deserves at least one memory like that.

Of course, I'm assuming the grandparent bar is there to seize, and increasingly it is. With 27% of all American children living in single-parent homes in 2010, it is the grandparents who are doing a lot of the parenting while the single parent holds down a job, if there's a job to hold. A few blocks from us lives a heroic couple raising their six-year-old granddaughter because her father is in prison and the mother has abandoned her. A hundred years ago, it's likely this innocent, now the legal ward of her grandparents, would have landed in an orphanage, but with American life expectancies approaching eighty, the majority of children born today will not only know their grandparents but their great grandparents as well.

One thing that continues to mystify me though is how poorly most parents get along with their sons' families relative to their daughters'. Even though my wife's parents lived in Germany while our two children were growing up, they enjoyed a warmer relationship with them via the telephone than with my English-speaking parents who often lived within driving distance. Sadly, the same is true today, for my wife and I have a better rapport with our daughter's family than we have with our son's. Indeed, in the great majority of cases we know of, the same is true. Too often, some friction between mother-in-law and daughter-in-law reaches the flash point, and the victims are the children. I recall seeing a bumper sticker in south Florida reading, "Ask me about our estranged grandkids." If my experience is widespread and my math is correct, roughly half of all grandchildren are disaffected.

The relatively recent appearance (c. 1920) of what I call the "third generation" has led to the poverty of idioms and proverbs alluding to grandparents. "Grandfather clock" is solidly ensconced even as the clocks are disappearing. But "don't teach your grandmother to suck eggs" is making a rapid exit probably because of the salmonella risk and the plastic eggs that need no sucking. In Great Britain, misers are sometimes described as people who would "dig up their grannies to steal the coppers from their eyes," but this expression began fading with the death of the large English penny and cremation's popularity. "Granny glasses," a rimless, unisex accessory that gained currency in the 1960s, is one of the few positive phrases I've located, but it's rarely used anymore. Pejorative phrases like "granny knot" implying ineptitude, or "grandfather clause" implying something devious or underhanded, appear to be firmly rooted. In recent years, "the grandaddy of them all" (the oldest of anything), "granny dumping" (abandoning the demented elderly in an emergency room), "granny farm" (an assisted living complex), and "granny flat" (a small addition to an existing home) have entered the language, but there aren't many more like them. The only proverb I'm aware of is the conservative motto, "What's good enough for grandfather is good enough for me."

Except for humans, lions, pilot whales, baboons, and some warblers, the "third generation" does not exist in the animal kingdom for the simple reason that most creatures of the field, sea, and sky do not live long enough. When that generation does exist in a species, it's usually the older females that stay home to supervise the children while the "second generation" hunts and gathers. Incidentally, among human hunter-gatherers, it's the plant-and-insect-gathering females who supply up to 70% of the calories at any given potluck meal. Though there are conflicting studies of the "grandma hypothesis," the extra productivity of the women and the relative safety of gathering may have given them the edge in longevity.

Whether man or beast, the "third-generation's" role is principally one of "first-generational" child tending, though in hard times, an economic support role often emerges. For males, the appropriate role usually consists of finding ways to be useful around the house without being a nuisance. For myself, I have fixed bike flats, helped to build a tree house and a deck, paint a bathroom, patch some sheetrock, and read to the children. When our grandsons want to shoot basketball, I am their somewhat-mobile backboard. My wife's chief role at our daughter's home is to take over the cooking and baking duties, but she has to be very careful not to do too much while visiting our son lest her assistance be seen as a criticism of our daughter-in-law's domestic competence or a ploy to reclaim her husband. Perhaps her safest role in either household is to serve as the "Grandmama-razzi," seizing only two-dimensional memories, no hostages. It's a delicate set of scales, and equilibrium does not come easy.

It's been said that you don't really understand a problem until you can solve it for your grandparents, but it seems the reverse is also true. Fortunately, my wife's mother was an excellent role model and problem solver; indeed, she wrote the "manual." Though she lived some five thousand miles away from our children when they were growing up, she was the one whose visits our children looked forward to and the one our children went to visit when they came of age. I'll cite one example of her transcontinental love. Four weeks before each Christmas, a large package arrived from our sainted Mutti (German for "Mom"). In the box was an Advent calendar for each of her grandchildren. On an embroidered sheet of green felt were twenty-four small gifts individually wrapped and tied to a gold ring sewn to the felt. It didn't take long before we all came to appreciate just how much effort and love had gone into that undertaking. With two more grandchildren at home, Mutti had ninety-eight gifts to buy, wrap, attach, and distribute. The gifts are long gone, but I still have one of the exquisite string knots she tied her parcel with. It's pinned to the wall over the table where we wrap our own gifts because that's our "manual."

Judging the Potato by Its Vine: Appearances

"Botox: the fun of rigor mortis without the inconvenience of death."
—Randy Cohen

"[Gray hair and wrinkles] are the hard-won credentials of my humanity."
—Eleonora Duse

Pelicans flying from Baja California over Arizona sometimes confuse the heat-shimmering highways with rivers. Attempting to land, they may break a leg or wing. Ornithologists can't be sure about the birds' misapprehension, but if they're right, it helps to explain the cripples that turn up in animal shelters during the annual migrations.

Pelicans aren't the only creatures in the animal kingdom fooled by appearances. Suicide was virtually unheard of in Native American communities until smallpox and mirrors were introduced by Europeans in the seventeenth century. Those few Iroquois and Algonquin who survived the disease received another setback when they saw themselves clearly for the first time in a silver-backed mirror. The scarred faces were often more than many could bear, and they jumped from the nearest cliff.

Surface appearance ranks low on the scale of things that matter, but it does count. When our son, Shane, was in the ninth grade, he took a course at my suggestion in woodworking. Over the year, he framed a picture, made a tie rack, and for the final project, built a bar stool of solid cherry. Over several weeks, he reported on how the project was progressing until finally he brought it home in a large plastic bag. He was beaming as he pulled the wraps off, but when I saw the finished product, my jaw dropped: there was dry glue running from most joints, and the four leg braces had each been set at unique angles, not one of which was horizontal. Even a blind man would have had to grit his teeth to live with this white elephant even if it was solid cherry. My wife said it had "character," and I agreed, while thinking "character assassination perhaps."

A week later, the shop teacher and I had a brief discussion. I said, "If Shane's project was an A, what does an F look like?" The teacher said shop classes today were more about self-esteem than craftsmanship. I was ready for that, but my wife said we needed to move on. "Self-esteem built on stools such as Shane's," I said as she dragged me off, "is a house built on sand," but I don't think he heard me.

If eyewitnesses are as unreliable as psychologists tell us, it behooves humans to use all their resources, not just their vision. After several elevator rides with Dean Morris Cox, the once gentlemanly academic who'd hired me, I hastily concluded that his social graces were waning with age. Often when I said "good morning," usually on a crowded elevator, he ignored my greeting. One day, I noticed a thin, flesh-colored wire running along the side of his neck. Suspecting a hearing aid, I asked a colleague, who'd known the dean longer than I had, if my hunch was well grounded. "Oh, yes," he said, "in a crowd, Morris is deaf as a stone."

A short time later, I nudged my wife at a concert and pointed out a man sitting below us who was sleeping. When the philistine rose at the end of the concert, he took a younger woman's arm, who was unfolding a white cane. The sleeper was blind, and so was I.

Evidently, I'm a slow learner, for perhaps a week later, I was riding the elevator to the eighth floor in the building where I work. A woman I recognized only as one who worked in the dean's office got on at the second floor and pushed "3." I said half in jest, "You ought to be ashamed of riding one floor." Icily, she replied, "I had a hip replacement a few months ago." Suddenly, I was very glad we had only one floor to ride together. Three times in two weeks, I'd been hoisted by the petards of my snap judgments.

But back to the dean who is ninety-five now and long retired. Not long ago, I had the pleasure of interviewing him for an oral history that the Clemson University Emeritus College is compiling. With fresh batteries and clean tubes in his hearing aids, Morris understood every question and responded in perfect paragraphs, which has been his conversational style for the forty years I've known him. Toward the end of our video-taped conversation, I tried to lighten things up, so I asked the heir to the Mt. Olive Pickle fortune about his Rolls-Royce. "Yes, Skip, if you must know," he said, "I do have a jar of Grey Poupon in the glove compartment." Then quite unexpectedly, he volunteered that an odd thing had happened a few years ago: he'd been traveling alone in his Rolls and had not shaven in several days. He was wearing garden shoes and old clothes because he'd been searching some rugged land a friend owned in the North Carolina mountains for some wildflowers that he hoped to transplant to his garden in Clemson. On his way home, he stopped at a country grocery to quench his thirst. While standing in line waiting to pay for a soda, the customer in front of him dropped a dime. Among the most honorable of men I know, Morris picked it up and offered it to the owner. Scanning his benefactor from head to toe, the customer said, "Keep it; you need it more than I do." Without a word, Morris paid for his purchase, returned to his Rolls, and prepared to leave. As he was driving off, the customer appeared again knocking on the driver's-side window. Perplexed, Morris braked and rolled down his window. Said the rude fellow, who'd finally recognized the Silver Cloud, "I want my dime back."

I've never driven a Rolls, but several years ago my wife and I bought a car that felt every bit as plush: a Toyota Camry. On one rearview mirror, however, was etched, "Objects in mirror are closer than they appear." I mention this because it was the first time I'd ever seen this inscription, and it led to a discussion of just how safe such a convex mirror might be in a high-speed situation. We were just beginning to get the hang of this questionable innovation when news came that my wife's father had died.

For months after the funeral, Ingrid and I helped her widowed mother through some serious depression, but before long, my dear wife slipped into the slough herself. Looking in the Camry's mirror one day, I had an idea. Early one morning, I wrote the following, "Objects in mirror are more beautiful than they appear" and taped it to her convex make-up mirror. Something apparently clicked because when I went to shave, I found a Post-it that read, "Objects in this mirror are smarter than I realized." Though it was a modest start, her cheerful self began to rematerialize.

An American proverb reads, "The blind man's wife needs no paint." True, if she lives in the wilds of Alaska and has no mirror, otherwise she needs her "paint" as much as suburbia's "desperate housewives." As the church has known for centuries, sustenance lies in illusion. Take the horizon, for example, a natural illusion, but a useful one to a traveler. Without it, trips longer than about three miles in treeless climes will appear endless and, therefore, difficult to undertake.

But judgments based on appearances, illusory or otherwise, remain risky. As Thoreau said, they're a lot like Walden's delicious ice whose bluish tinge was seen by consumers as a sign of impurity while the "white ice" of Cambridge tasted of weeds. Too often, it seems, we "shop" with our eyes alone.

A Note on the Author

Born December 12, 1941 at Walter Reed Hospital in Washington, DC, Skip is the son of Dorothy and Sterling Eisiminger. In 1959, he graduated from Mt. Vernon HS (his tenth school in twelve years). In 1963 while serving three and a half years in the Army Security Agency, he married Ingrid Barmwater of Helmstedt, West Germany. With her committed assistance, he graduated from Auburn University in 1967 (BS) and 1968 (MA). The same year, he settled his family in Clemson, SC after taking a job teaching English and interdisciplinary humanities at Clemson University. After his son Shane was born in 1964 and his daughter Anja in 1969, he returned to graduate school in 1970. In 1974, he graduated from the University of South Carolina with a PhD in English after which he returned to Clemson, where he looked forward to most Mondays until his retirement in 2010. His only move after his return was across town. Over forty-two years in academe, he published a book of verse, a book of word games, a children's book, and two collections of essays. In forty-two years as a teacher at Clemson, he taught over nine thousand students in twenty-nine different courses.

A recovering Presbyterian, Skip's firmest belief is in the illusion of free will. As a poet, he's aware rime does not pay; as an essayist, he knows it's not the eloquence but the evidence; as a critic, he assumes the best until he knows otherwise; as a linguist, he prides himself on being an ento-etymologist (a debugger of words); as a teacher, he has discovered if he makes the material seductive, the students will teach themselves; as an employee, he usually completed the worst first; as a husband, he comes to the table with something to share, and as a father and grandfather, he is a carpet bonder. Gradually, he has come to understand the virtue of giving more and expecting less, and that while curiosity did kill the cat, he has several more.